Δ The Triangle Papers: 39

Latin America at a Crossroads:
The Challenge to the Trilateral Countries

A Report to
The Trilateral Commission

Authors: George W. Landau
President, Americas Society;
former U.S. Ambassador to Venezuela and Chile

Julio Feo
Chairman, Consultores de Comunicacion y Direccion;
former Chief of Staff to Prime Minister Felipe González

Akio Hosono
Chairman, Japan Association for Latin American Studies;
Professor, The University of Tsukuba

Associate Author: William Perry
President, Institute for the Study of the Americas

Published by
THE TRILATERAL COMMISSION
New York, Paris and Tokyo
August 1990

Library of Congress Cataloging-in-Publication Data

Landau, George W., 1920–
    Latin America at a crossroads : the challenge to the trilateral countries : a report to the Trilateral Commission / authors, George W. Landau, Julio Feo, Akio Hosono ; associate author, William Perry.
    56 pp.   cm. — (The Triangle papers : 39)
    ISBN 0-930503-62-7 : $6.00
    1. Latin America—Relations—North America. 2. North America—Relations—Latin America. 3. Latin America—Relations—Europe. 4. Europe—Relations—Latin America. 5. Latin America—Relations—Japan. 6. Japan—Relations— Latin America. I. Feo, Julio. II. Hosono, Akio. III. Trilateral Commission. IV. Title. V. Series.
F1416.N7L36   1990   90-42829
337.807—dc20   CIP

Manufactured in the United States of America

THE TRILATERAL COMMISSION

345 East 46th Street	c/o Japan Center for	35, avenue de Friedland
New York, NY 10017	International Exchange	75008 Paris, France
	4-9-17 Minami-Azabu	
	Minato-ku	
	Tokyo, Japan	

The Authors

GEORGE W. LANDAU assumed the presidency of the Americas Society and the Council of the Americas in July 1985, following a distinguished career in the U.S. Foreign Service. Ambassador Landau worked in the private sector from 1947 to 1957 when he entered the Foreign Service. He served as Commercial Attaché and Chief of the Economic Section in Montevideo, Uruguay, until 1962 and while there was a member of the U.S. Delegation at the meeting that created the "Alliance for Progress." From 1962 to 1965, Ambassador Landau was First Secretary and Political Officer in the U.S. Embassy in Madrid. He was the State Department's Country Director for Spain and Portugal in the Bureau of European Affairs from 1966 to 1972. In 1972 he was appointed Ambassador to Paraguay, where he served until 1977. From there he went on direct transfer as Ambassador to Chile, where he remained until 1982. He was Ambassador to Venezuela from 1982 to 1985. Ambassador Landau holds the rank of Career Minister in the Senior Foreign Service. He received the State Department's "Superior Honor Award" in November 1970 for his work in the negotiation on the 1970 Spanish Base Agreement and the 1971 Azores Basing Agreement with Portugal. He was awarded the "Presidential Meritorious Service Award" in 1984 and was decorated by the Governments of Chile and Venezuela. George Landau attended New York University, and graduated from George Washington University in Washington, D.C.

JULIO FEO is Chairman of Holmes & Marchant Group (España) and of Consultores de Comunicacion y Direccion. Mr. Feo studied political science at Madrid University and obtained an M.A. in International Relations and Political Science at Stanford University in the United States. He then worked at Columbia University in social research for three years. Since 1966 he has been involved in the communication industry. He was General Secretary in the Office of Spanish Prime Minister Felipe González from 1982 to 1987.

AKIO HOSONO is Professor at The University of Tsukuba and Chairman of the Japan Association for Latin American Studies. Educated at The University of Tokyo (B.A., 1962), Dr. Hosono was a staff member of the United Nations Economic Commission for Latin America and the Caribbean (ECLAC) from 1966 to 1976. With that long experience in

Latin America behind him, he organized a series of cultural and academic exchange programs between Latin America and Japan, and over the years he has been a great force in furthering the promotion of Latin American studies in Japan. He was a Lecturer then Assistant Professor at The University of Tsukuba before he received his Ph.D. in economics in 1984. From 1986 to 1988 he was head of The University of Tsukuba Center for Foreign Students. Dr. Hosono is author of *Latin American Economies* (in Japanese) (1983), *Mexico-Japan Relations: New Dimensions and Perspectives* (in Spanish) (1985), and *Structure of Latin American Crises: Future Directions of Debt Problems and Democratization Processes* (in Japanese) (1986).

WILLIAM PERRY (Associate Author), President of the Institute for the Study of the Americas, is a veteran Latin American specialist with two decades of experience in academia, in government service and in private consulting. He has written extensively on hemispheric affairs and other international topics for publications in Europe and Latin America, as well as the United States. Mr. Perry received his B.A. in History and Political Science from the University of Vermont, and he went on to earn an M.A. in Latin American Studies and International Affairs at the Wharton School of the University of Pennsylvania. Between 1971 and 1981, Mr. Perry taught or conducted research at the Foreign Policy Research Institute of the University of Pennsylvania, the School of Advanced International Studies of the Johns Hopkins University, the Stanford Research Institute and, in Brazil, at the Political Science and International Relations Department of the University of Brasilia. He returned to the United States in 1981 to direct the Latin American Program at the Center for Strategic and International Studies, while also serving as a consultant with the U.S. State Department and various multinational corporations. In February of 1985, Mr. Perry was invited to become chief staff member for Latin American affairs of the Senate Foreign Relations Committee. And he later served as Director for Latin American Affairs at the National Security Council. Immediately after leaving the government, Mr. Perry became Vice President of Neill and Company, a government relations firm, and served as Chairman for the working groups dealing with Latin America in the 1988 Presidential Campaign of George Bush. He assumed ISOA's presidency in May of 1988.

The Trilateral Process

The report which follows is the joint responsibility of its authors. Although only the authors are responsible for the analysis and conclusions, they have been aided in their work by many others. The authors are greatly indebted to William Perry, Associate Author, who has provided vital support—including major drafting support—throughout the project. The persons consulted spoke for themselves as individuals and not as representatives of any institution with which they are associated. Those consulted or otherwise assisting in the development of the report include the following:

Elliot Abrams, *Former U.S. Assistant Secretary of State for Inter-American Affairs*

Carmelo Angulo, *General Director, Institute for Latin America Cooperation, Madrid*

Alfredo Arahuetes, *General Secretary, CEDEAL (Latin America Study Center), Madrid; Assistant to Julio Feo*

Julio Arguelles, *Professor of Economic Structure and Latin American Economy, Complutense University, Madrid; Researcher, CEDEAL (Latin America Study Center); Assistant to Julio Feo*

Lloyd Axworthy, *Member of the Canadian House of Commons*

Norman Bailey, *President, Norman A. Bailey, Inc.; former Special Assistant to the U.S. President for International Economic Affairs, National Security Council*

Adrian Beamish, *Permanent Assistant Under-Secretary of State for the Americas, Foreign and Commonwealth Office, London*

Georges Berthoin, *European Chairman, The Trilateral Commission; International Honorary Chairman, European Movement*

John Bosley, *Chairman, Standing Committee on External Affairs and International Trade, Canadian House of Commons*

Max Cameron, *Assistant Professor, Carleton University*

Jaime Carvajal Urquijo, *Chairman, Iberfomento, Madrid*

Leycester Coltman, *Head of Mexico-Central America Department, Foreign and Commonwealth Office, London*

Geraldo da Costa Olanda Cavalcanti, *Ambassador of Brazil to the European Community*

Jeremy Cressmell, *Assistant Head of South America Department, Foreign and Commonwealth Office, London*

Russ Davidson, *Director-General, Caribbean and Central American Bureau, Canadian Department of External Affairs*

Guido Declercq, *Chairman, Investco, Brussels*

Tim Draimin, *Policy Director, Canadian Council for International Cooperation*

Julio Ego-Aguirre, *Ambassador of Peru to the European Community; former Chairman, GRULA (an association of Latin American Ambassadors to the European Community)*

Georges Fauriol, *Director of Latin American Program, Center for Strategic and International Studies, Washington, D.C.*

George Foulkes, *Member of British Parliament*

Garret FitzGerald, *European Deputy Chairman, The Trilateral Commission; Member of Irish Dail; former Prime Minister*

Andrew V. Frankel, *Assistant North American Director, The Trilateral Commission*

Ludlow Flower, *Managing Director, Council of the Americas; Vice President, Americas Society*

John Gilbert, *Member of British Parliament*

Stan Gooch, *Director-General, South American Branch, Canadian Department of External Relations; former Canadian Ambassador to Costa Rica*

Wolf Grabendorff, *Director, Institute for European-Latin American Relations (IRELA), Madrid*

Robert Graham, *Latin America Editor,* The Financial Times

Sir William Harding, *Director, Lloyds Bank; former British Ambassador to Brazil*

The Earl of Harrowby, *Chairman, Dowty Group; Chairman, The Private Bank, London*

Eikichi Hayashiya, *Advisor, The Mitsui Bank Ltd.; former Japanese Ambassador to Spain*

Charles B. Heck, *North American Director, The Trilateral Commission*

Miguel Herrero de Miñon, *Member of Spanish Parliament*

Takashi Hosomi, *Chairman, NLI Research Institute, Tokyo; former Chairman, Overseas Economic Cooperation Fund*

Sir Kenneth James, *Director General, Hispanic and Luso Brazilian Council (Canning House), London*

Noriaki Kishimito, *Senior Economist, Research Institute of Overseas Investment, The Export-Import Bank of Japan*

Paul Lejour, *General Delegate, Fabrimetal, Brussels*

Frederico Mañero, *Consultant, Comunicacion y Direccion, Madrid; former Director, Pablo Iglesias Foundation for Latin America*

Manuel Marin, *Vice President, Commission of the European Communities*
Abel Matutes, *Member of the Commission of the European Communities (in charge of Latin American affairs)*
Robert Miller, *Associate, Parliamentary Centre for Foreign Affairs and Foreign Trade, Ottawa*
Lord Montgomery, *Vice Chairman, Latin America Parliamentary Group in the House of Lords; President, Hispanic and Luso Brazilian Council (Canning House), London*
Makito Noda, *Senior Program Officer, Japan Center for International Exchange, Tokyo*
Yoshio Okawara, *Japanese Deputy Chairman, The Trilateral Commission; Executive Advisor, Keidanren (Federation of Economic Organizations in Japan); former Ambassador to the United States*
Sir Michael Palliser, *Deputy Chairman, Midland Bank, London; Chairman, Samuel Montagu & Co.*
Jaime Paz Zamora, *President of the Republic of Bolivia*
Carlos Andrés Perez, *President of the Republic of Venezuela*
Luis Guillermo Perinat, *Member of Spanish Parliament*
Susan K. Purcell, *Vice President, Latin American Affairs, Americas Society, New York*
Ross Reid, *Member of the Canadian House of Commons*
John Reimer, *Member of the Canadian House of Commons*
Paul Révay, *European Director, The Trilateral Commission*
John Robinson, *Vice President, Americas Branch, Canadian International Development Agency*
John Roper, *The Royal Institute of International Affairs*
David Rockefeller, *North American Chairman, The Trilateral Commission*
Phil Rourke, *Parliamentary Centre for Foreign Affairs and Foreign Trade, Ottawa*
Guadalupe Ruiz Gimenez, *Secretary-General, AIETI (Association for Research and Study of Ibero-American Issues), Madrid; Member of European Parliament*
Javier Ruperez, *Member of Spanish Parliament*
Jutaro Sakamoto, *Director-General, Central and South American Affairs Bureau, Japanese Ministry of Foreign Affairs*
Peter Shore, *Member of British Parliament*
Christine Stewart, *Member of the Canadian House of Commons*
Marqués de Tamarón, *Director, Centre for Foreign Policy Studies, Madrid*
Sir Peter Tapsell, *Member of British Parliament*
Geoffrey Taylor, *Chairman, Daiwa Europe Bank, London*
David Thomas, *Advisor of Overseas Scholarships Funding, London*

SCHEDULE OF TASK FORCE ACTIVITIES:

April 1989 — Draft terms of reference prepared.

May — Feo comments on terms of reference.

September 12 — Perry prepares outline.

September 15-16 — Landau, Feo, Perry and Flower meet in New York City to discuss outline and broad thrusts of report.

September 22 — Feo meets in Brussels with Belgian members, EC officials and experts, and diplomats posted to the European Community.

October 29 — Feo discusses report with European members assembled in London for regional meeting.

November 16 — Hosono meets in Tokyo with Trilateral Commission Chairmen, Deputy Chairmen and Directors, and with Japanese experts; and submits paper on relations of Trilateral countries, especially Japan, with Latin America.

December — Perry completes first draft.

January 9-10, 1990 — Landau, Feo, Hosono and Perry meet in Madrid to discuss first draft and meet with Spanish members, officials and experts. Feo submits material on Europe-Latin America relations and for policy recommendations chapter.

January 29-30 — Feo meets with British members and experts in London.

January-February — Hosono and Feo submit additional material.

February 23 — Perry meets with Canadian members and experts in Ottawa.

March 15 — Perry completes second draft.

early April — Third draft completed˅and circulated to Trilateral Commission members.

April 18-20 — Authors participate in Trilateral Commission discussions with Mexican leaders in Mexico City.

April 21 — Draft report discussed at annual meeting of the Trilateral Commission in Washington, D.C.

late June — Final draft completed for publication.

Summary of Policy Recommendations for the Trilateral Countries

Political

1. Sustained, high-profile public support for democracy in Latin America must comprise the cornerstone of Trilateral foreign policy toward the region. This includes:

   - more frequent consultation and more intense association with the democratic leaders.

   - strengthening of links between kindred political parties of the industrialized countries and the nations of the region.

   - expanded private and government-sponsored exchange programs to foster democracy and enhance understanding with the Trilateral countries—with special attention to individuals from parliaments, the press, academia, the military, government bureaucracies and the private sector.

   - increased support for programs aimed at improving the local administration of justice—in order to promote equity, improve public safety and foster a modern regulatory climate. E.C. nations with kindred legal systems, especially Spain and Portugal, could be particularly helpful in this regard.

2. Special and sustained efforts should be made to work closely with local governments on problems caused by threats to regional democracy and the continued existence of recalcitrant, undemocratic regimes.

Economic

1. With due deference to local circumstances and sensibilities, the Trilateral countries should be frank in advocating the need for reform and modernization of Latin American economies. Such efforts are necessary both to achieve recovery and secure international support—particularly from the Trilateral private sector.

2. On the other hand, the Trilateral countries must be prepared to provide simultaneous and effective debt relief on a case-by-case

basis for Latin American nations making a real reform effort. This will involve:

- more Mexico-like arrangements for reform-minded governments—tailored to local circumstances on a prompt, sequential basis.

- greater coordination among international financial institutions, Trilateral governments and private credit institutions. In particular, the European Community should consider greater channeling of credit resources through the Inter-American Development Bank. For example, the linking of the European Investment Bank to the Inter-American Development Bank should be seriously considered.

- review of Trilateral countries' laws and regulations on amortization of debt write-down and on loan-loss reserve requirements.

- consideration of greater and more timely contributions to international financial institutions—based upon their respective policy performance.

- encouragement of debt-equity swaps as appropriate to local circumstances.

- support for modernization and strengthening of local capital markets and programs like Employee Stock Ownership Programs (ESOPs) that encourage wider equity ownership.

- consideration by those Trilateral nations with large trade surpluses of Japanese-style capital recycling efforts. Reduction of Trilateral budget deficits, especially in the case of the United States, would also contribute to greater availability of credit for Third World nations, including those in Latin America.

3. The Trilateral nations should keep their markets open to Latin American products to the greatest extent practicable. The Trilateral countries should:

- support Latin American countries' efforts to promote exports to Trilateral countries, especially non-traditional exports to non-traditional markets, and explore opportunities for reducing trade barriers where Latin American countries have greatest comparative advantages. This latter point applies most particularly to Japan and those E.C. nations still experiencing trade surpluses with the region.

- consider undertaking bilateral trade-barrier reduction initiatives on a reciprocal basis—like the present U.S.-Mexican framework agreement and the discussions of a possible free trade area that are now underway.

- support expansion and strengthening of the Caribbean Basin Initiative (CBI) concept.

- in the case of Western Europe, consider granting of Lomé privileges to more regional countries; and, more generally, turn over more responsibility and authority for Latin American trade matters to E.C. bodies.

- encourage regional free trade initiatives and integration efforts (such as prompt reconstitution of the Central American Common Market) and greater Latin American participation in trade with Eastern Europe and the Pacific Rim.

- press for reinvigoration of the GATT process and/or a move toward new general world trade initiatives. Special attention here should be devoted to manufactured exports of special interest to the region, like textiles and steel—and, of course, to the reduction of protectionism in agriculture in the Trilateral nations.

4. The industrialized nations should also keep Latin American investment opportunities well in mind. The Trilateral countries should:

- stress the need to foster a favorable local business climate.

- devote adequate attention to OPIC-like insurance guarantees and bilateral investment treaties that assure potential investors.

- regularly dispatch investment missions to keep regional opportunities in full view of Trilateral private sectors.

- promote more active use of in-bond industry and joint-production efforts between Trilateral and Latin American countries—both to utilize local labor and transfer technology to the region.

- consider tax and other incentives for private sector investment in debtor nations.

5. Trilateral aid levels to the region must be kept at the highest practicable levels, and these funds must be used in the most effective possible manner. The Trilateral countries should:

- ensure that the percentage of total Trilateral aid flows destined for Latin America is as great as possible.

- aim these funds carefully at truly productive projects or real human needs.

- take full advantage of volunteerism and PVOs.

Foreign and Security Policy

1. Prudent, realistic attention must be devoted to a changing constellation of regional security issues.

   - The first and preferred option is close support of local efforts toward stability and security.

   - The development of a more effective regional security system should be encouraged, for collective defense of local democracies and protection of their citizens against criminal violence. This implies fundamental rethinking of the OAS and the Rio Treaty and their relationship to NATO.

   - Closer police and legal cooperation is needed on the drug question among the Trilateral countries and between them and the region. The Trilateral countries should consider support for regional police establishments—including the possibility of a standing regional force.

   - The Trilateral nations should also urge regional actors to adher to the Nuclear Non-Proliferation Treaty and to exercise restraint in the transfer of weapons systems that might aggravate conflict in other areas of the globe.

2. A positive and more concrete policy agenda should be forged between the Trilateral and Latin American countries. The Trilateral countries should:

   - foster greater integration of the Latin American democracies in the councils of the industrialized world.

   - cultivate a climate of respect, realism and reciprocity.

   - actively search for grounds for positive mutually beneficial cooperation in key areas like trade, finance, natural resources, the environment, law enforcement—and collaboration in multilateral organizations.

   - consider channeling new worldwide environmental protection initiatives toward the Latin American countries.

Table of Contents

I. INTRODUCTION

The purpose of this report is to assess the present and future importance of the Latin American-Caribbean region[1] to the remainder of the international system and adduce the resultant policy implications for the Trilateral countries. Toward this ambitious end, it will be necessary to describe the present circumstances of the region and identify the salient trends which are transforming it. Then the stakes and principal issues for the industrial democracies—singly and in concert—require assessment. Finally, reasonably specific policymaking imperatives for the United States, Canada, the E.C. countries and Japan (and, implicitly, for the nations of the region) must be distilled. The purpose of this effort is to help Trilateral policymakers find a place for the societies of Latin America and the Caribbean in the future international order—one which offers the maximum benefits and entails the fewest difficulties, both for them and for the peoples of the industrialized democracies.

Latin America long subsisted on the margin of the wider currents of international affairs. Indeed, its discovery and settlement were part of the process by which the newly dynamic European state system consolidated its dominant influence around the globe. As colonial holdings of Spain, Portugal, Great Britain, France and Holland through the 18th Century, the lands of the region basically provided resources for, and venues of, conflicts having their origin at the core of a Eurocentric world. Even after the majority of regional societies achieved their independence at the beginning of the 19th Century, their internal difficulties, weakness and remoteness made them objects rather than actors in a world order centered, first, on London and, later, Washington.

On the other hand, looking back over the broad sweep of history, the nations of the region seemed to recover from the nadir of their

---

[1] For our purposes, the Latin American-Caribbean region (sometimes abbreviated as Latin America) embraces all those nations stretching from the Rio Grande and the islands of Caribbean Sea to Tierra del Fuego. The extreme heterogeneity of the area and the non-Latin character of many of its component parts are well-recognized by the authors—indeed, highlighting of this fact will comprise one of the salient themes of this work. But our audience knows this region as Latin America and for reasons of clarity and convenience we will succumb to this convention.

fortunes in the middle of the 19th Century and be moving gradually, if sometimes erratically, toward a more autonomous and respectable position in the mainstream of the international community. Substantial economic and social development created an increasingly modern, capable and self-confident constellation of societies. And, in more recent years, even general movement toward realization of long-illusive regional aspirations to democratic government seemed in train.

At the same time, no foreign actor any longer dominated the region. Most local nations had acquired substantial autonomy in international affairs and the various poles of power in the wider world actually seemed to be in competition for the attention of Latin American and Caribbean nations. Indeed, certain local states had begun to forge a role for themselves beyond the confines of the region. Furthermore, the combination of development within the region and progressive integration of the global community brought all local societies into much closer contact with the remainder of the international system.

Thus, the promise seemed bright that Latin America would eventually realize its long-latent potential—to its own benefit and to the distinct advantage of the industrialized democracies. The socio-economic crisis that has become apparent over the course of the past decade, however, casts a shadow over this process and even threatens to reverse its course. As a result, Latin America stands at a portentous crossroads. Given both our direct stakes in the region and the considerable role that it will surely play in future world affairs, the Trilateral nations can not afford to be oblivious to the path which is chosen.

II. Current Circumstances and Trends

Latin America is a huge area of almost 7 million square miles, stretching from the southern borders of the United States some 6,000 miles to the Antarctic. Thus, it is not much smaller than the whole Trilateral world, taken together. The region's rapidly growing population, now above 400 million, is among the more developed components of the so-called Third World. Moreover, its enormous wealth of both human and natural resources holds out great promise for the future. But its problems come on an equally colossal scale.

The first thing to be noted is that Latin America is not, in many respects, a homogeneous region at all—but rather a collection of countries and sub-regions having far less in common than most outside observers imagine. The nations of the Southern Cone, for example, bring to mind the societies and historical experience of Spain and Italy; Barbados could easily be mistaken for a black constituency in England; and Haiti might be more logically located in West Africa than in the Caribbean Sea. Mexico, Central America, Panama, the non-Latin Caribbean, Cuba, the Andean countries and Brazil each possess unique characteristics and obey their own dynamics. In addition, it is extremely important to remember that, as groups, the nations of the Caribbean, Middle America, the Andes and southern South America deal far more with the United States and Europe directly than they do with each other. With all this said and understood, it is still possible—and necessary—to make some general observations on present circumstances and trends throughout the region.

There is much to be said in a positive vein. Decades (in some cases, over a century) of economic and social development have produced a substantial modern component to almost all local societies that can compete effectively with counterparts around the globe. Regional economies grew, internationalized and diversified to a remarkable extent during past decades. Particularly since the Second World War, new generations of scientists, administrators, businessmen and politicians have emerged that could lead their countries to realization of their developmental objectives and full participation in the future course of world history. The last colonies in the Caribbean have achieved and maintained their independence and the practice of democratic government has made remarkable progress throughout the region—especially during the last decade. In fact, with the exception of Cuba, all the countries of the region are now either practicing democracies or apparently on the way to that universal objective. Old-fashioned, dysfunctional statism and economic xenophobia of the 1960s and 1970s—increasingly seen as bankrupt and discredited—are clearly in retreat, and the appeal of revolutionary Marxism is at low ebb.

There is, however, also a decidedly negative side to this balance sheet. The progress of some sectors of these societies has increased and made more apparent the traditionally wide gap between rich and poor in the region. At the same time, these disadvantaged elements are becoming progressively politicized and are being called upon to participate in their newly democratic systems of government. While old economic ideas may have been intellectually discredited, new and more promising approaches have not necessarily been effectively implemented. And many nations find themselves stuck along the desired path toward political modernization, economic growth and wider social opportunity.[1] Change of the magnitude Latin America is undergoing—and the frustration caused by insufficiently rapid realization of growing expectations—have let fester, spawned or aggravated a host of ills, including grinding poverty, gross lack of elemental social infrastructure, abuse of the environment, corruption, and violence.

These ills have been greatly aggravated by the generally adverse economic circumstances brought on by local mismanagement and a series of external shocks. The past decade has been characterized by debilitating debt burdens, capital flight, reduced investment, economic stagnation—and the perverse spectacle of these developing countries consistently exporting considerably more capital than they are receiving. The 1980s, in fact, have been something of a lost decade so far as Latin America's socio-economic development is concerned.[2] The social consequences of this tragic situation, in terms of poverty, crime and emigration are plain for all to see. And the political repercussions of these unsustainable circumstances are now clearly beginning to manifest themselves.

---

[1]As Table 1 indicates, only five Latin American countries had a higher real per capita GDP in 1988 than in 1980. Eleven stood lower in 1988 than they did in 1980, six lower than they did in 1970 and three lower than they did in 1960.

[2]"Has It Been a Lost Decade?," *The IDB Newsletter* (September-October 1989), pp. 8–9.

TABLE 1
Per Capita GDP of Latin American Countries
(1988 U.S. dollars)

Country	1960	1970	1980	1988*	
Chile	1,845	2,236	2,448	2,518	
Argentina	2,384	3,075	3,359	2,862	(<1970)
Uruguay	2,352	2,478	3,221	2,989	(<1980)
Brazil	1,013	1,372	2,481	2,449	(<1980)
Paraguay	779	931	1,612	1,557	(<1980)
Bolivia	634	818	983	724	(<1970)
Peru	1,233	1,554	1,716	1,503	(<1970)
Ecuador	771	904	1,581	1,477	(<1980)
Colombia	927	1,157	1,595	1,739	
Venezuela	3,879	4,941	5,225	4,544	(<1970)
Guyana	1,008	1,111	1,215	995	(<1960)
Surinam	887	2,337	3,722	3,420	(<1980)
Mexico	1,425	2,022	2,872	2,588	(<1980)
Guatemala	1,100	1,420	1,866	1,502	(<1980)
Honduras	619	782	954	851	(<1980)
El Salvador	832	1,032	1,125	995	(<1970)
Nicaragua	1,055	1,495	1,147	819	(<1960)
Costa Rica	1,435	1,825	2,394	2,235	(<1980)
Panama	1,264	2,017	2,622	2,229	(<1980)
Dominican Republic	823	987	1,497	1,509	
Haiti	331	292	386	319	(<1960)
Jamaica	1,610	2,364	1,880	1,843	(<1970)
Trinidad & Tobago	3,848	4,927	8,116	5,510	(<1980)
Barbados	2,000	3,530	3,994	4,233	
Bahamas	8,448	10,737	10,631	11,317	

Source: Inter-American Development Bank, *Economic and Social Progress in Latin America, 1989 Report* (Washington, D.C.: IDB, 1989), Table B-1, p. 463.

*preliminary information

The security situation in Latin America and the Caribbean presents a mixed picture. In general terms, there is little prospect of purely national conflict among the countries of the area or between them and any extra-regional powers. The great majority of local governments do not face an imminent threat of revolution. But certain deadly and dangerous situations continue to be cause for grave concern, especially in Central America and the Andean area. The Cuban question is still a matter for regional concern. Terrorism remains a serious problem and criminal violence, especially that which is linked to the spreading scourge of the drug trade, is on the rise. In fact, in some cases, alliances between insurgents and drug traffickers have come to threaten the very existence of civilized society and democratic government—notably in Colombia and Peru. Moreover, the specter of popular unrest and military reaction hangs over many of the new and still weak democracies. And, overall, the region lacks a coherent and effective arrangement to protect itself from very real threats to its values and interests.

Latin America's position in the wider world also presents a disparate blend of positive and negative elements. The long-standing demands of local actors to chart their own foreign policy courses have largely been met. At no time in history have so many local nations realized their aspirations to democracy and international acceptance. Nor has there been a time when the winds seemed to be blowing so strongly in favor of democracy around the globe. Most regional leaders must be pleased that the East-West conflict, which they often decried for submerging North-South issues, is abating. And a largely prosperous international community seems to offer considerable economic opportunity for those with the will and wit to grasp it.

Yet the nations of Latin America and the Caribbean find themselves immersed in serious difficulties and seem unsure of how to insert themselves into the international context. Most regional foreign policies seem merely ritualistic and, increasingly, overtaken by events. In part this is due to heightened preoccupation with serious domestic problems. But, as far as critical questions of development are concerned, the region's traditional Third World rhetoric seems hollow and sterile. Perennial calls for regional solidarity are not matched by real cooperation on a substantial and realizable agenda geared to forwarding the concrete interests of local societies. In short, much of the region appears to be increasingly left behind and marginalized by the fast-flowing course of international events. However, Mexico, Bolivia, and Chile are among those nations which are abandoning the straitjackets of the past to embark on the bold new initiatives—particularly economic initiatives—appropriate to present and future demands on the region. The real challenge of the 1990s is the quest for definitive insertion of Latin America and the Caribbean into the competitive/cooperative framework of the growing community of the developed democracies.

III. THE STAKES FOR THE TRILATERAL COUNTRIES

The world we have all known is in the process of rapid and profound change. The course of recent events holds forth the prospect of an end to the sometimes bloody and always dangerous East-West strategic competition that has characterized the post-World War II period. It offers hope that the nations of Eastern Europe, and perhaps even the Soviet Union itself, may be gradually incorporated into the global community of developed democracies.

The Trilateral countries cannot fail to be gratified by this process and active in our efforts to bring about its full realization. At the same time, we must be realistic and should not lose either our sense of proportion or our interest in other world areas which will inevitably play an important role in the new world order taking shape out of current changes. Latin America has about three times the population of Eastern Europe and, even in its present depressed and semi-developed state, over twice Eastern Europe's GNP. In terms of natural resources and long-term socio-economic potential, the disparity is far greater. Moreover, while we may entertain hopes for democracy growing in the eight countries of Eastern Europe, it has already emerged in the overwhelming majority of the more than 30 nations of Latin America and the Caribbean. In an inherently unforeseeable future, who is to say where the greatest gains for human freedom and well-being may now be made? While the policymakers of the Trilateral nations attempt to cope with the crucial passage which Eastern Europe is now transiting, they should not forget that Latin America also stands at a great historical juncture.

A. The United States

For the United States, of course, the Western Hemisphere has always been an area of unique and fundamental importance. Although sometimes neglected among Washington's other wide-ranging priorities, Latin America and the Caribbean are certain to play an even more crucial and obvious role in U.S. foreign relations than they have in the past. Because it is the great power of the Hemisphere, the

United States finds it difficult to avoid becoming involved in intra-regional diplomacy and the political contention that often transfixes the nations of the region. There now exists a strong bi-partisan consensus in the United States that active support of the area's long-standing aspirations toward democratic government offers the best guarantee of stability in, and cooperation from, the region. Thus, both U.S. values and U.S. interests are closely engaged in the fate of the regional democracies and, by the same token, in the controversies that are attendant to their creation and sustenance.

Although somewhat diminished from decades past, the United States remains the principal foreign economic presence in the region as a whole.[1] The U.S. private sector has about $80 billion of direct investment in the area.[2] Meanwhile two-way trade totalled over $90 billion during 1988 (see Table 2). In addition, the U.S. government sends the region some $2.5 billion in economic aid annually and is the largest financial backer of such regionally significant multilateral institutions as the Organization of American States, the Inter-American Development Bank, the International Monetary Fund and the World Bank.

The past decade has produced somewhat disappointing results in terms of U.S.-Latin American economic relations. Investment levels and trade have stagnated, significant numbers of U.S. jobs have been eliminated through lost exports, and large loans are at risk. In addition, constant controversy seems to attend trade, debt and investment questions. On the other hand, the United States receives real benefits from its ongoing relationship with Latin America.[3] Initiatives like the *maquiladora* program, the CBI and general tariff

---

[1]In general, the predominance of the United States in the foreign trade of Latin America declined during the late 1960s and the 1970s. Japan, intra-Latin American trade and the rest of the Third World gained percentage-wise during this period. The crisis of the 1980s, however, has reversed the diversification trend. In rough terms, the United States accounts for 40 percent of the region's trade in more recent years, the European Community about 20 percent, intra-Latin American trade about 15 percent, and Japan around 5 percent. The big losers in the 1980s have been intra-regional commerce, trade with the Third World and trade with the European Community. Japan has remained more or less steady. See Inter-American Development Bank, *Annual Report 1988* (Washington, D.C.: IDB, 1988), pp. 114–115; GATT, *International Trade '87-'88*, volume II (Geneva: GATT, 1988), appendix table AA10; and Table 2 of this report.

[2]Dependable and comparable investment figures are very hard to determine. Direct U.S. investments tend to be older and, for tax purposes, are kept at book value, thus serving to understate their current market value. The U.S. Department of Commerce, the Association of American Chambers of Commerce in Latin America, and the Council of the Americas gave the authors figures ranging from 50 to 80 billion dollars.

[3]As Table 2 indicates, only in 1987 did total U.S. trade with the region recover to pre-1982 levels. Despite depressed conditions in Latin America, U.S. exports to the area in 1989 were considerably greater than those to Japan, and roughly equivalent to those destined for West Germany, Great Britain, and France combined. International Monetary Fund, *Direction of Trade Statistics* (Washington, D.C.: IMF), various monthly issues from 1989 and 1990.

TABLE 2
Trade of Trilateral Areas with Latin America
(billions of U.S. dollars)

	1981	1982	1983	1984	1985	1986	1987	1988
United States								
Exports	39.66	30.80	22.14	23.74	26.35	26.86	36.08	44.73
Imports	37.88	35.39	38.08	44.30	40.49	31.70	43.41	47.78
European Community								
Exports	22.90	16.64	12.32	12.38	13.16	16.58	20.04	20.75
Imports	23.29	22.23	21.78	22.56	22.33	18.78	20.35	24.76
Japan								
Exports	7.66	6.19	3.70	4.01	4.31	5.25	6.11	6.50
Imports	5.00	4.95	4.97	5.30	5.11	4.63	5.23	6.61
Canada								
Exports	2.84	2.26	2.00	2.11	1.77	1.67	2.06	2.29
Imports	3.39	2.65	1.87	2.28	2.03	1.56	2.55	2.92

Source: The numbers for 1982-88 are from the International Monetary Fund's *Direction of Trade Statistics Yearbook 1989* (Washington, D.C.: IMF, 1989), pp. 44 and 46. The 1981 numbers are from the 1988 *DOTS Yearbook*.

reduction offer substantial prospects of enhancing trade, promoting reform and, most significantly, heightening U.S. competitiveness.[4] And no industrialized country would benefit so much from a recovery of the economies of Latin America as would the United States.[5]

The 1990 census will show upwards of 20 million U.S. citizens of Latin American and Caribbean descent. In addition, somewhere between five and ten million people from the region are in the United States on an extra-legal basis. Thus the United States is now, in a population sense, the fifth largest Latin American nation—a fact which brings with it a host of advantages and some serious difficulties.[6] Local turmoil plus improved transportation and communications links bring all citizens of the region—and their problems—closer to the United States. Immigration has consistently benefitted U.S. society and the recent wave of Latin arrivals is, in general, no exception. But extremely large, extra-legal and potentially inassimilable flows can cause resentments, burden social services, and spawn criminality.

Drug trafficking has also emerged as a very significant issue during recent years. U.S. society spends billions of dollars in an effort to police its borders and help foreign countries intercept unwanted individuals and cargoes, the vast majority of which come from Latin America. A recent study funded by the federal government estimated that drug abuse costs U.S. society some $60 billion annually.[7]

The United States also inevitably gets involved when threats emerge to its own regional security interests or those of friendly local nations. This has particularly been the case when the Soviet Union or Cuba figure in the equation—or, as was the case of Panama, when some tangible and politically sensitive asset is at risk. In recent years the United States has been heavily absorbed in the ongoing Central

---

[4]The *maquiladoras* (also often referred to as in-bond industries) are plants in Mexico that perform assembly or packaging operations for U.S. companies and are taxed only on the value added by such activities—i.e., the movement of these goods in and out of Mexico is not treated like imports and exports. They provide substantial employment in Mexico while enhancing the price-·competitiveness of U.S. industry. The Caribbean Basin Initiative (CBI) is a package of legislation passed by the United States Congress in 1983 that basically extends, with some exceptions, duty-free treatment to goods produced in Central America and the Caribbean, and permits certain *maquiladora*-like operations in this region as well.

[5]A healthy and growing Latin America would probably help alleviate the chronic U.S. trade deficit and might serve to take the edge off contention between the United States and its Trilateral partners, especially Japan. See Peter Drucker, "Help Latin America and Help Ourselves," *The Wall Street Journal* (March 20, 1990).

[6]Only Brazil, Mexico, Colombia and Argentina have larger populations than the estimated 25–30 million people who now reside in the United States and trace their ethnic roots to the region.

[7]"The Cost of Drug Abuse: $60 Billion a Year," *New York Times* (Dec. 5, 1989), p. D1.

American crisis. And new difficulties are clearly developing in places like Colombia, Peru and, perhaps, Haiti. To cope with these situations the United States maintains considerable security forces at the ready and provides approximately $1.5 billion per year in military assistance to its regional allies. (The United States is also a significant vendor of arms to the region, although its position has been greatly undermined in recent decades by extra-hemispheric competitors and burgeoning local arms industries.)

B. The E.C. Countries
The ties of the European Community countries with the region go back, of course, to the very origins of contemporary Latin American societies. Discovered and colonized by Britain, France, the Netherlands and, especially, Spain and Portugal, today's Latin America is an adaptation of European civilization to the conditions of the New World—and, in varying degrees, to the native cultures the Europeans found there and the African elements that they brought in their train. Language and culture are the most obvious manifestations of this process. But Latin American politics, government, economic practices and foreign policy outlooks are also strongly influenced both by the traditions of the respective mother countries and by more contemporary European thought and experience. Personal links and persistent immigration patterns over the years have served to reinforce the relationship.

The scope and nature of ties with Latin America varied greatly, of course, among the diverse nations of Europe which later became the European Community. Their regional empires were extremely important to Spain and Portugal, although basically in terms of maintaining the metropole's competitive position in Europe. With regard to Britain, France and Holland, this was much less the case—and for other European nations Latin America hardly mattered at all.

In any event, the decline of Spain and Portugal within the European state-system and the independence which most of Latin America achieved in the early 19th Century markedly reduced the region's significance for most of Europe. The *Pax Britannica* of that century, enforced by the British fleet, discouraged continental thoughts of recolonization and allowed England to achieve predominant economic influence throughout most of the region. Thereafter, the expanding power of the United States gradually established an "Inter-American system" under the economic and political leadership of Washington, which reached its apogee in the immediate post-World War II period.

European ties with the region were by no means completely extinguished, however, by the gradual emergence of U.S. predominance in the Hemisphere. Britain long retained significant Caribbean colonies and maintained a strong economic presence, especially in the Southern Cone. France, in addition to occasional imperial adventures, was a respectable trading nation and a leader in cultural and intellectual terms. Germany evolved into a significant economic and technological partner for certain Latin American nations and, bolstered by a steady stream of immigration, entertained thoughts of challenging the U.S. position during the two World Wars. Even Italy developed something of a presence, by dint of strong patterns of immigration to Argentina and other Latin American nations.

Spain, of course, also continued to have a unique role vis-à-vis most of the region, as did Portugal with respect to Brazil. Although much less important economically and politically than the United States or the major European powers, the Iberian states continued to occupy a significant place in the cultural, social and foreign relations of regional states (also buttressed by persistent patterns of immigration).

Recovered from the Second World War, largely divested of its colonial ties and newly linked in the European Community, Europe, from the 1960s on, has experienced a sharp renaissance of its role in the world and with respect to Latin America. During the 1960s and 1970s, trade, lending and investment relations with Latin America grew rapidly. Growing European political influence logically followed and was welcomed by most Latin American nations as a hopeful sign of recognition of the region's growing role in the world and as a useful counterweight to Washington. The return of Spain and Portugal to the mainstream of European life and their integration into the European Community capped this process and provided Latin America with eager advocates at the center of an increasingly integrated European decision-making process.

During the course of the 1980s, however, the region's political and economic difficulties and seemingly brighter opportunities in other parts of the world have reduced overall European attention to Latin American affairs. But the E.C. countries retain both a substantial stake in the crucial passage that the region is now transiting and significant capabilities to affect its ultimate outcome.

European political institutions have made a strong commitment to Latin America's still fragile experiment in democracy. The principal political parties of the E.C. nations (and their respective foundations) are at the forefront of the effort to strengthen the practice of democracy in the region and the local institutions that support it. The machinery of the European Community itself has also been active in this regard. And, of course, the individual European governments would much prefer to deal with stable, effective and democratic counterparts in Latin America rather than the all-too-obvious alternatives. The success of Latin American efforts to reinvigorate their economies and institutionalize pluralistic democracies would mark a long step forward toward the kind of world order that most Europeans would like to see. It might also provide some useful models for the crucial process now going on in Eastern Europe. But failure in Latin America would be a disaster, with disquieting implications for other areas of the Third World with which the European Community is even more closely linked. Also, of course, Europeans know that political turmoil in Latin America often distracts the United States from the role that they believe Washington should play vis-à-vis Europe and other issues of broader international concern.

European economic interests in Latin America are also substantial. Collectively, the E.C. nations have about $32 billion in direct investment throughout the region in a wide variety of enterprises. The continued prosperity of Europe, of course, depends, to a large extent, on international commerce. And, in this area, total trade turnover is upwards of $45 billion per year, despite the evident stagnation of the past decade (see Tables 2 and 3). At the same time, Europe has a very real stake in the debt question as it has reference to Latin America. Not only are the European nations substantial contributors to the large international lending institutions, but they also hold considerable Latin American debts directly as well. Moreover, the private banking sectors of the E.C. countries, when taken together, face exposure which is at least as great as that of their American counterpart. As presently situated, the companies and credit institutions of Europe have much to lose if the Latin American economies continue to deteriorate. And they might expect to benefit considerably if this trend could be reversed.

In social and personal terms most European nations have not been greatly affected by events in Latin America. But Spain, Portugal and, to a certain extent, Italy do have close human ties with the region. Moreover, drug trafficking from the area is a problem of growing European concern. And the prospect of increasing immigration levels in the future is not to be discounted.

With regard to Latin American security questions the general level of European concern and propensity for involvement is low. But there

TABLE 3
Trade with Latin America
of European Community Countries and Norway
(billions of U.S. dollars)

	1981	1982	1983	1984	1985	1986	1987	1988
				Federal Republic of Germany				
Exports	6.02	4.51	3.23	3.26	3.80	4.94	6.21	5.91
Imports	4.10	4.00	3.99	4.12	4.30	4.79	4.57	5.77
				France				
Exports	3.78	3.25	3.01	2.71	2.70	3.63	4.65	5.13
Imports	3.08	2.88	2.75	2.74	2.53	2.10	2.32	2.89
				Italy				
Exports	2.94	2.44	1.38	1.43	1.47	1.88	2.20	2.64
Imports	3.90	3.69	3.07	3.11	3.18	2.16	2.62	3.01
				United Kingdom				
Exports	3.63	2.15	1.65	1.92	1.92	2.18	2.38	2.47
Imports	2.53	3.02	3.00	3.39	2.87	2.31	2.65	2.97
				Spain				
Exports	1.93	1.71	1.05	0.99	1.11	1.14	1.28	1.47
Imports	3.49	3.13	2.88	2.90	2.99	1.88	2.39	2.57
				Netherlands				
Exports	1.48	1.18	0.95	0.92	1.02	1.21	1.47	1.29
Imports	3.92	3.39	3.80	3.68	4.09	3.26	3.21	4.24
				Belgium/Luxembourg				
Exports	0.85	0.72	0.50	0.63	0.58	0.76	0.94	0.82
Imports	1.23	1.19	1.45	1.60	1.40	1.30	1.50	1.95
				Denmark				
Exports	0.52	0.48	0.42	0.46	0.37	0.51	0.63	0.74
Imports	0.42	0.35	0.35	0.32	0.39	0.48	0.55	0.61
				Portugal				
Exports	0.10	0.07	0.04	0.04	0.05	0.14	0.07	0.08
Imports	0.35	0.36	0.33	0.51	0.37	0.29	0.31	0.51
				Ireland				
Exports	0.18	0.11	0.08	0.10	0.13	0.17	0.19	0.18
Imports	0.05	0.06	0.04	0.06	0.07	0.06	0.07	0.09
				Greece				
Exports	0.06	0.02	0.01	0.01	0.01	0.02	0.02	0.02
Imports	0.22	0.16	0.12	0.13	0.14	0.15	0.16	0.15
				Norway				
Exports	0.32	0.18	0.11	0.15	0.18	0.20	0.22	0.33
Imports	0.28	0.28	0.25	0.30	0.29	0.31	0.33	0.29

Source: The numbers for 1982-88 are from the International Monetary Fund's *Direction of Trade Statistics Yearbook 1989* (Washington, D.C.: IMF, 1989), pages 44 and 46. The 1981 numbers are from the 1988 *DOTS Yearbook*.

are exceptions, including the residual regional holdings and commitments of Britain, France and the Netherlands—of which the Falklands-Malvinas war was a dramatic reminder. Some European nations have exported considerable quantities of armaments or technologies with military implications (including nuclear technologies) to the region. Others are engaged in joint production of hardware or other equipment with potential military uses. At the same time, certain sectors of European opinion and governments, especially the Spanish, take an active interest in the Central American crisis. And occasionally there are more general worries about the degree to which U.S. involvement locally may affect what, for Europe, are the more central concerns of trans-Atlantic security.

In general E.C. foreign policy terms, the salience of Latin America has declined over the course of the past decade. On one hand, the economic crisis that has gripped the region serves to reduce European expectations of material gain from an enhanced relationship with Latin America. And, on the other, internal E.C. concerns and new foreign opportunities, especially with regard to Eastern Europe, clearly have taken center stage. Seemingly interminable problems in, and with, Latin American countries have certainly dimmed European hopes that the region might emerge any time soon as another pole of power in the world of developed democracies.

At the same time, the E.C. nations should remain conscious of the enduring importance of the region and the critical historical juncture at which it now stands. Rhetorically, there is still recognition of these realities in most European capitals. And important political support does come from Europe for the struggling democracies of the region and local efforts to achieve peace and stability. Aid levels, both from governments and private groups, are reasonably generous. And some collective steps have been taken, such as the admission of Haiti and the Dominican Republic to the benefits of the Lomé Convention. The Portuguese government and, especially, the Spanish government have, naturally, been at the forefront of the struggle to keep an appropriate degree of European attention focused on Latin America.

But a great deal remains to be done, by individual European governments, by E.C. institutions and by the E.C. nations in cooperation with other developed democracies having important stakes in the region. This is particularly true with respect to trade and debt issues. A great deal also depends upon the Latin American nations, which need to make strong efforts both to reform their local economies and to hold onto their fair share of European attention in an age of conflicting new priorities.

C. Japan

Over the long course of history, geography, culture and international politics have tended to isolate Japan from Latin America. During recent decades, however, the Japanese have, with characteristic energy, forged a significant but still secondary position in the region, especially in the economic realm. These new ties are based upon a naturally complementary relationship between a Japan which is increasingly well-endowed in terms of capital, technology and management and a region which is abundant in natural resources and opportunities for their development. And they are supplemented by a pattern of immigration which has made Latin America the most considerable locus of Japanese settlement outside the home islands. Over one million people of Japanese origin now live in the region, with particular concentration in Brazil.

Neither too much nor too little should be made of Japan's presence in the region. Its trade numbers do not compare with those of the E.C. nations, taken as a whole, or, certainly, with those of the United States. By the late 1980s Japan's two-way trade with the region came to about $13 billion annually (see Table 2). The level of direct investment is now put by Japanese officials at $32 billion (although a significant component of this investment is in flags-of-convenience shipping, insurance and other off-shore operations[8]). Trade with Latin America is only about 4 percent of Japan's total international commerce, but the region was the locus of some 17 percent of its overseas investment as of the end of 1988. As is the case for all the industrialized democracies, Japan's trade and investment relationship with the region has stagnated, declining relative to rapid growth elsewhere during the course of the 1980s.[9] Even for Latin America, as a whole, overall Japanese trade and investment to date is not hugely significant. Still, Japan's numbers are more than comparable with those of any single European nation. Moreover, they are significant for particular countries—notably Brazil and Mexico and, more

---

[8]According to Akira Aoki, Deputy President of Japan's Export-Import Bank, $22.4 billion was in these off-shore types of activities. "New Directions in Japanese Financial Cooperation in the Region," paper delivered by Mr. Aoki at the Fourth Symposium on Financial and Business Cooperation between Latin America and Japan, Nagoya, Japan, November 12-14, 1989, p. 4.

[9]The value of trade between Japan and Latin America expanded at a rate of 15 percent annually during the 1960s and 19 percent during the 1970s—but has stagnated during the past decade. Ibid., p. 3.

recently, Chile—and especially concentrated in the most dynamic sectors of the region's economies.

In addition, Japan has assumed an important role as a creditor to Latin America, both directly and through its burgeoning role in multilateral lending institutions. The Japanese government is itself a significant factor in this regard. And private Japanese banks had about $44 billion in medium- and long-term loans outstanding as of March 1988, placing them in second position, behind U.S. institutions, among Latin America's commercial creditors. A considerable amount of Japan's overall exposure was incurred through its efforts to cooperate in implementation of various international debt relief initiatives.

Japan's interests in Latin America are almost exclusively economic in nature. The lustre of Latin America's promise as a region of great opportunity has dulled in recent years. But Japan still wants access to the region's significant natural resources and food production capabilities—and has found that the area has potential as a platform for exports to the United States. In general, Tokyo shuns involvement in regional security questions and attempts to avoid local political controversies. Likewise, it does not desire contention with its major allies and trading partners—especially the United States—over a region which for it is of secondary importance.

There was a time, in the 1970s and early 1980s, when Japan was sometimes criticized for lack of development assistance to Latin America comparable with either its growing capabilities or emergent interests in the region. In truth, Tokyo's aid priorities, traditionally concentrated in East Asia, did lag behind its emerging trade, investment and credit relationship with Latin America. Since that time, however, some significant changes have been made.

The global total of Japanese foreign assistance levels doubled in U.S. dollar terms between 1983 and 1987. Furthermore, a $50 billion foreign aid program was announced for the five-year period beginning in 1988, making Japan among the largest dispensers of purely economic aid in the world. More recently, the Japanese government has shown particular interest in channeling funds toward projects aimed at contributing toward the solution of global, as well as local, environmental problems.

In addition, the Japanese government has embarked upon a plan to recycle, between 1987 and 1992, some $65 billion of its extraordinary trade surpluses to provide credit for heavily indebted nations and is becoming markedly more involved with multilateral lending institutions. These moves and the articulation of the

Miyazawa initiative in 1988 (a precursor of the Brady Plan, announced six months later) show the Tokyo government's predisposition to contribute to resolution of the region's ongoing debt crisis. Japan obviously possesses both specific interests in the region and an appreciation of the general role that it plays—and could come to play—in ensuring a healthy economic world order. Moreover, Tokyo has made available resources capable of making an important contribution to the recovery of the economies of Latin America and the Caribbean. At the same time, Japan recognizes the more fundamental importance of the region to others, especially to the United States.

Japan's prosperity and generally positive disposition may not necessarily result in immediate strengthening of the economic relations between Latin American countries and Japan. The Japanese banks and business community, in general, have soured on the region's prospects as a whole. Where regional nations have something concrete to offer—in Mexico and Chile, for example—Japanese capital has not shown hesitation. But only after stable and positive conditions are created in the region will private Japanese capital and technology flow more generally at the rates that they did in the 1960s and 1970s.

For the present and generally speaking, it is apparently Tokyo's intent that the government take the lead while the companies follow cautiously—or simply hold back. Japanese authorities exhibit a willingness to cooperate with others in an effort to help Latin America help itself out of current difficulties. But this would require a coordinated effort involving all the concerned industrialized democracies and the local actors themselves.

D. Canada

Historically, the countries of Latin America have not been central to Canada's foreign policy concerns. But there has long existed a strand of interest in the affairs of the region which now appears to have developed into a positive and decided facet of contemporary Canadian foreign policy.

A trading relationship, especially with the Caribbean, dates back centuries. And these links were supplemented by a limited number of significant Canadian investments, notably in the mining and utilities sectors, in certain South American countries. In addition, joint membership in the British Commonwealth resulted in a somewhat special relationship between Ottawa and the English-speaking states of the Caribbean.

At a more personal level, Canadian missionaries (not to mention tourists) have long had a significant presence in the region, especially in the lands bordering the Caribbean Sea. More recently, the Montreal area has come to attract a substantial community of Haitian immigrants. And a substantial number of, often church-related, grassroots organizations have developed strong concerns over the turmoil which has convulsed Central America—while this same crisis has resulted in a certain amount of legal and illegal immigration from the Isthmus. Drug trafficking from the region is also a growing issue in contemporary Canadian society.

Favorable international circumstances and the desire of the Trudeau government to diversify from Canada's historical focus on Great Britain and the United States resulted in a marked quickening of economic ties with the area during the 1960s and 1970s. And, although these links have not been immune from the vicissitudes of the 1980s, Canada retains a respectable level of involvement in the economic affairs of the region. Canadian direct investment in the area approaches $2 billion, and two-way trade between Canada and Latin America is now in the $5 billion range on an annual basis (see Table 2). In recent years, Canada has generally run a trade deficit with the region, facilitating Latin America's efforts to earn the hard currency it so desperately needs. Private Canadian banks, however, once considerable lenders to the region, have substantially liquidated their commitments and show little sign of renewed interest.

The recent course of domestic and international events has led many Canadian politicians and the Mulroney Government to rethink the country's historically diffuse relationship with Latin America. And the conclusion, in the words of Foreign Minister Joe Clark, is that it is time for Canada "to find a home in the Americas."[10] Canada's historical ties with Europe, the Commonwealth and other Third World areas—and, of course, her very substantial ties with the United States, especially in the context of the new free trade agreement—will continue to consume the lion's share of attention. But Canada is now apparently committed to a serious, if discreet, policy toward the remainder of the Western Hemisphere that is symbolized by its 1989 decision to formally enter the Organization of American States (OAS).

Given their traditions, Canadians are obviously pleased by the wave of democracy that has swept Latin America in recent years and

---

[10]The phrase comes from Mr. Clark's definitive speech on "Canadian Policy Towards Latin America" delivered in Calgary on February 1, 1990, and widely disseminated by the Canadian Ministry of External Affairs.

hopeful at the signs that the crisis in Central America may now be abating. The government obviously wants to work harmoniously with the United States, while avoiding involvement in the often controversial regional difficulties to which Washington is often subject. A peaceful and democratic Latin American environment in which both Washington and Ottawa can work together toward positive ends is manifestly the Canadian preference.

And Canada has valuable, if somewhat limited, roles to play in this regard. In the first place Canada enjoys an excellent and unencumbered reputation in Latin America. Any efforts it can make to support democratic government and the institutions which make its practice possible would be well-received in the region. And Ottawa can credibly aspire to be viewed as an independent and honest intermediary between Washington and Latin American nations, especially at such regional fora as the OAS and the Inter-American Development Bank.

Canada's economic assistance budget is limited and, for the present, still skewed toward Africa and Asia. In the last fiscal year, in fact, Canadian foreign assistance to the region was $340 million, only 16 percent of its total foreign aid.[11] But, hopefully, this share will gradually increase over time. And Canada does have funds and experience which, if properly concentrated, can have a significant impact in particular cases. Moreover, the private giving habits and volunteerism of Canadians is truly impressive and these human and financial resources also have a positive role to play.

The Canadian economy is a powerful development vehicle which could be more effectively harnessed to the needs of Latin America, but certain limitations must be kept in mind. Canada itself is, in substantial measure, a raw material and agricultural exporter. And its industries will be pressed to compete under the new accord with the United States. Moreover, Canadian trade with the region has stagnated in recent years due to the adverse economic situation that has obtained there—while the nation's investors and bankers have become somewhat soured on its prospects. But surely one way to diversify Canada's economic ties and enhance Canadian competitiveness would be through increased trade and joint-venture operations with the nations of Latin America. Canadian and Mexican officials are already discussing the implications of increasingly close U.S.-Mexican trade arrangements for Canada. This matter should be

---

[11]Official Development Assistance (ODA) figures received directly by authors during interviews in Ottawa, February 23, 1990.

fully explored with a positive disposition. And additional ways should be actively sought to spur exports to the region while examining protectionist facets of Canadian trade legislation to see if new opportunities for regional imports can be found.

Canada has little interest in involving itself in hemispheric security questions. It does not provide any security assistance at all as a matter of policy. And its entrance into the OAS specifically did not encompass membership in the Inter-American Defense Board. Canada is, however, disposed to participate in worthwhile peace-keeping forces under the aegis of appropriate international organizations, as its stellar record in this regard around the globe attests.

In short, while a relatively modest player in Latin America compared to the United States and the great trading nations of Europe and Asia, Canada has a potentially valuable role to play—especially in the political realm. Moreover, the Canadian government has recently come to the firm decision to take a more active and concerted role in its own Hemisphere. In charting their collective course toward Latin America, all Trilateral countries should take full cognizance of Canada's new disposition and unique capabilities.

IV. The Issues of the 1990s and Beyond

Present circumstances and trends place Latin America at a portentous crossroads in the region's historical development. The Trilateral countries possess a clear and vital stake in the outcome of this process. What, then, are the dimensions of the principal issues which both local nations and concerned foreign powers will have to address effectively during the course of this decade?

A. Political

The major political question that confronts local societies, now and for the foreseeable future, is whether they can achieve and maintain workable forms of democratic government. Democracy in this context means not only valid periodic elections, but also good faith efforts toward observation of basic human rights and freedoms and the realization of a substantial measure of social justice. It also means a government that is able to function effectively, peaceably adjudicating domestic differences of opinion and implementing policies which are of real benefit to local societies.

The historical problems of democracy in Latin America are well-known. Each country, of course, has its own unique story. But most of these nations have spent the bulk of this century oscillating between periods of often unstable elected government and military rule. In general terms, this pattern has tended to be cyclical for the region as a whole. The Great Depression of the 1930s brought a wave of authoritarian regimes, which receded in the immediate post-war period. And another cycle of military rule began in the 1960s, only to be terminated over the course of the past decade.

There are, of course, many partial—and even some complete—exceptions to this generalization. For example, Mexico formed its own unique civilian semi-authoritarian antidote to these cycles. Costa Rica established a new democracy in the late 1940s that has continued uninterrupted since that time. Both Venezuela and Colombia experienced military dictatorships in the 1950s, but moved toward democracy thereafter and withstood the later swing of the pendulum.

The Caribbean is, of course, another story altogether. The older independent states of Cuba, Haiti and the Dominican Republic followed their own unique rhythms. And a host of new parliamentary governments emerged from colonial status beginning in the 1960s, appeared to weaken in the 1970s, and then largely recovered their equilibrium in the 1980s.

The wave of democracy which characterized the 1980s has now created an unprecedented number of freely elected civilian governments in the region. As of the present moment, only Cuba has completely resisted the tide. All the other countries of the region, comprising well over 90 percent of its population, are ruled by governments that are substantially democratic or making perceptible progress in that direction. But, at the same time, it should be borne in mind that in certain cases, like Colombia, the social and institutional bases for democracy are being undermined by the corrosive impact of criminality and violence.

The central political question is how democracy will fare in the 1990s and beyond. Can the nations of the region repair the deficiencies that traditionally caused democracies to collapse? What new challenges face today's democracies and can they cope with these as well? Are there any changes in structure or practice that will have to be undertaken in order for them to survive and prosper? Are returns to military rule, violent radicalism or new and even more insidious forms of authoritarianism in the future of regional nations? What about cases of chronic anarchy, criminality, gross repression, or subversion of neighboring democracies? What are Latin American democracies and the Trilateral countries to do in cases of political regression?

An adequate response to these questions is difficult to provide. Much of the answer lies in the hands of the citizens of Latin America and the Caribbean themselves. The political culture of the region must be modernized in order to instill values of tolerance, realism and efficiency that are necessary for democracy to survive anywhere. All sectors of society—business, labor, the press, intellectuals, and even the armed forces—must find their place within workable democratic frameworks. And the system must work—providing fair adjudication of disputes and adequate policy direction, while allowing and encouraging private initiatives and institutions to perform their fundamental role. This, in turn, will require courageous and capable leadership from politicians and political parties.[1] At base, these efforts will have to be undertaken by local societies themselves. Still, the prospects for the success of such necessary efforts will be affected by events in the wider world. And the degree of support which is provided by important outside actors could prove a decisive factor.

B. Economic

The underlying economic question facing the nations of Latin America and the Caribbean is whether they are able to forge updated systems of production capable of meeting the material needs of their societies and supporting their peoples' legitimate social and political aspirations. Such economic systems must be competitive in a liberalized world economy. And they must be able to produce strong, sustained patterns of growth, while distributing—and being perceived to distribute—the fruits of this expansion in a reasonably equitable manner.

There are some real regional success stories and there exist many positive trends and bases of hope for the future. But it is equally true that an abundant number of failures and grounds for deep concern can be found. Each country of the region is its own combination of achievement and frustration. In general terms, however, it is an unquestionable fact that the region, as a whole, faces a very profound economic crisis, the resolution of which comprises the basic challenge of the 1990s.[2]

This crisis involves two inter-related sets of factors. International circumstances hit Latin America hard during the 1980s. But, even more fundamentally, they revealed long-festering flaws in the region's economic institutions and its whole conceptual and policy approach to the question of development. Local politicians and intellectuals first tended to focus on the external causes of the region's economic difficulties. Gradually, however, both they and their foreign

---

[1]Bolivia, for example, was once thought to be a nearly hopeless case. In spite of a history of chronic political instability, severe social problems and an apparently overwhelming economic crisis (which sent inflation rates to five digits), the Bolivian political class rose to the challenge. Between 1985 and 1989 a de facto coalition between the traditionally left-of-center PNR and the conservative ADN both preserved that nation's fragile democratic institutions and implemented a tough and effective program of economic reform. As one of the poorest nations in Latin America, Bolivia still has its problems. But this experiment was so successful that it has been renewed under the present administration of President Jaime Paz Zamora, whose historically far-left MIR is likewise cooperating with the ADN.

[2]Latin America's real GDP expanded almost 70 percent in the decade of the '60s, nearly 80 percent in the decade of the '70s—but only about 10 percent between 1980 and 1988, an increase that was more than offset by population growth. See Inter-American Development Bank, *Economic and Social Progress in Latin America, 1989 Report* (Washington, D.C.: IDB, 1989), p. 463.

counterparts seem to be recognizing that the roots of dysfunction lie deep within the region, its governments and its development policies—as well as in equally real external difficulties.

By and large, the economic traditions of Latin America can be traced to the mercantilist practices of the former colonial rulers—traditions which always meant a great deal of governmental-bureaucratic involvement in local economies. During the 19th Century, dire necessity, bright opportunities (for some) and foreign pressure opened them to foreign capital and technological inputs—particularly from Great Britain and the United States. As a result, when and where stability prevailed in the region during that often troubled century, economic growth was considerable—and in some cases spectacular.

Given the nature of local societies and then prevailing international norms, the bulk of the wealth that was generated went into the hands of regional governments, the resident elite and foreign entrepreneurs. But a great deal of productive infrastructure was laid down, substantial capital was accumulated and, where local social and political circumstances permitted, relative prosperity ensued. In most cases this liberal period lasted through the first three decades of the 20th Century, that is, until the Great Depression brought it to a crashing halt.

Many of the world's economic powers compromised formerly dominant liberal principles during this cataclysm—and some came to reject them altogether. Not surprisingly, Latin America largely followed suit. It is also important to note that this all came about at the same time that the nations of Latin America—especially the larger and more advanced countries—were experiencing substantial politicization of the, heretofore, inert masses of their population. The end of traditional elite-group dominance, economic collapse and a recoiling of the Great Powers from classical liberalism (indeed, the emergence of Communism and National Socialism, and other varieties of Fascism in Latin Europe) all occurred more or less simultaneously. And their effect on Latin American economic thought and practice was considerable.

The post-war period brought a renaissance of democracy and renewal of intense economic contact with the wider world economy. But it also witnessed the continuing politicization of local societies which gave rise to broad-based nationalism and redistributionist economic currents of thought. The decolonization process elsewhere in the world produced a host of new nations which shared Latin

America's continuing underdevelopment. And "development economics" became the universal antidote for the region's problems, with the state as the central director of the process.[3]

Under this scheme of things, high protective tariffs were erected to protect the governments' new developmental initiatives. Nationalizations were frequent, new state companies were created, local entrepreneurs were made concessionaires of the state, and foreign investment was strictly regulated, where it was not discouraged or proscribed. Central bureaucracies expanded enormously in terms of their size, spending and role in directing the remainder of society.

All this was made possible because Latin America had done well during the war years and because capital was abundant. It came from foreign companies, initially anxious to expand during the post-war prosperity, and from new international lending institutions. Some foreign governments provided direct foreign aid and, as these sources stagnated in the 1970s, lending from private banks became available.

The oil shocks of the 1970s, the international recession of the early '80s and the debt crisis finally burst this bubble. But productive foreign investment had long since begun to dry up and local capital flight had reached alarming proportions well before the bankers served notice. The debt burden and low commodity prices are real enough phenomena, but they must be added to the basic problem of what, by the 1970s, most of the economies of the region had become.

The situation varied, of course, from country to country—depending upon each nation's experience, resources and particular policies. But, in general terms, the effects were similar, varying only by degree. High tariffs and non-tariff barriers had frequently become a permanent crutch for inefficient industries, which provided consumers with shoddy goods at high prices—while discouraging their managements from entering new, more productive areas of endeavor. Many state companies evolved into large white

---

[3]In Latin America this strand of thought is most closely associated with Dr. Raúl Prebisch. During the 1950s, Prebisch developed and popularized the idea that constantly deteriorating terms of trade between Latin America's raw material and agricultural exports and the manufactured goods imported from the industrialized world required the nations of the region to develop their own industries and pursue strongly protectionist policies of import substitution. In some minds, these notions hardened, during the 1960s and 1970s, into a neo-Marxian, *dependentista* school of thought, positing a positive plot by the capitalist "metropole" to keep Latin America in its thrall at the "periphery" of the international economic system. Toward the end of his long life, Dr. Prebisch himself came to question the practical consequences of many of the concepts that had made him famous.

elephants, producing poor goods and services (or little result at all) at enormous cost to local governments and taxpayers.[4] Huge, cumbersome, and in some cases corrupt, bureaucracies further swelled government deficits, while serving largely to obstruct legitimate and potentially productive new initiatives.

High budget deficits produced chronically high rates of inflation which robbed the poor, encouraged capital flight and reduced investment—except in areas "guaranteed" by the government. Restrictions on foreign capital also constrained fresh capital inflows and discouraged the introduction of new, more competitive technologies. Low levels of productive investment aggravated unemployment, which governments were pressured to soak up with additional expensive programs and projects.

All this cost money that was not coming into the treasury because of the unproductive nature of the process—and because of various forms of corruption, of which massive tax evasion was clearly one. Thus, there was progressive recourse to borrowing (and the printing of money)—first from relatively permissive foreign governments and multilateral lending institutions, then from banks charging commercial rates, and finally from individuals and institutions willing to purchase short-term government paper only at truly extraordinary rates of interest. More and more loans were needed, in a progressively addictive syndrome, just to keep fundamentally unproductive institutions afloat. Eventually the finite amount of capital available to the region for such purposes was exhausted and the bubble burst in the debt crisis of the 1980s.

Clearly the world recession of the early 1980s and the high real interest rates that prevailed thereafter contributed to the ultimate result. And, obviously, the current weight of the debt burden—foreign and domestic—precludes rapid recovery from what has become a deep, decade-long recession. But it is important to realize that the practices which reached full flower in the 1970s were not, in the long run, sustainable in an increasingly competitive global economic

---

[4]The nationalized Argentine railroad system is a good example. It is widely acknowledged to have four or five times the number of employees that it needs, tracks and rolling stock are in bad condition, and service is poor and undependable. Moreover, many individuals have, through bureaucratic or personal favoritism, secured passes which allow them to ride for free. The losses, which are reported to run between two and three million dollars per day have, over the years, required substantial borrowing to sustain. And the Argentine government (and people) now have heavy principal and interest payments due for a service that is substantially inadequate. This situation was well understood by the government of Raúl Alfonsin and is a matter of grave concern to the present Menem Administration. Neither has been able to do anything about it, however, because of residual nationalism and the resistance of the powerful railway workers' union.

environment. And even substantial alleviation of present external burdens will be unavailing if fundamental changes are not made at the local level.

The current level of the debt burden afflicting regional governments and societies is staggering and, in most cases, comprises an insuperable obstacle to economic recovery and adequate servicing of pressing social needs.[5] This is not just a question of the interest payments—at historically high real international rates—on the $400 odd billion foreign debt (see Table 4). It also has increasing reference to the burden imposed by even higher rates of interest paid on *domestic* indebtedness, which has grown at an alarming rate in recent years.[6]

In a more general sense, the region simply needs more capital than it is generating, receiving and retaining.[7] The current crisis not only imposes the burden of debt service, but also severely restricts access to new loans for potentially productive purposes. Under current circumstances Latin American nations can only get substantial new credits in deals reached when disaster is impending. By that time the monies are usually earmarked for service of prior obligations or to prop up institutions that are on the verge of collapse.

Moreover, current conditions are obviously not conducive to new investment and, in fact, both foreign and local capital tend to flee the region when they are able. This means not only an insufficiency of funds for productive investment, but also a loss of new management and technological inputs that are necessary to keep the productive infrastructure of regional nations competitive with those of other areas around the globe.

On the trade side of the equation, the nations of Latin America and the Caribbean face serious problems selling the goods that they do

---

[5]For a summary of trends on the debt front and the problems remaining, see the Summary Report of the conference on New Initiatives on Latin American Debt, held at the Institute of Politics of the John F. Kennedy School of Government, Harvard University, on May 15–16, 1989.

[6]Brazil and Mexico, probably because they have the most developed securities markets in the region, have the most serious problems in this regard. By way of example, the Brazilian government, because of its chronic budget deficit and its inability any longer to borrow abroad, has had increasing recourse to the sale of substantial quantities of short-term paper on the local "overnight" market. To attract the money it needs, it must pay very high real interest rates. Thus, although the Brazilian government has not been servicing its foreign debt in recent months, its interest payments are almost as high as ever because of increasing domestic borrowing.

[7]According to Inter-American Development Bank statistics, Latin America experienced a net outward resource transfer averaging $27 billion a year in the 1983–87 period. Because these numbers do not take into account unrecorded flows, like under-invoicing of exports and surreptitious capital flight, they substantially understate the magnitude of the problem. Inter-American Development Bank, *Annual Report 1988* (Washington, D.C.: IDB, 1988), p. 116.

TABLE 4
Latin America's External Debt and Debt-Service Ratios, 1981-91*

	1981	1983	1985	1987	1989	1990[†]	1991[†]
Total External Debt (billions of U.S. dollars)	288.8	344.4	369.1	415.9	398.6	407.5	416.7
By maturity							
short-term	50.6	47.1	27.0	35.5	39.6	33.1	31.3
long-term	238.3	297.3	342.1	380.4	359.0	374.4	385.4
By type of creditor							
official	n.a.	48.3	67.6	98.1	109.4	120.2	137.2
commercial banks	n.a.	244.5	255.5	271.1	246.3	242.1	235.1
other private	n.a.	51.6	46.0	46.7	42.9	45.2	44.4
Total External Debt							
as % of GDP	39.8	46.8	45.4	43.7	36.7	35.0	32.9
as % of exports of goods and services	209.8	291.6	295.6	344.6	271.6	264.4	250.3
Total Debt Service							
as % of exports of goods and services	43.9	42.7	41.3	35.9	35.1	35.2	36.1
Interest Payments							
as % of exports of goods and services	24.5	30.6	29.4	22.0	19.9	24.5	21.9

Source: International Monetary Fund, *World Economic Outlook, May 1990* (Washington, D.C.: IMF, 1990), Tables A46, A48, and A49. The 1981 numbers are from the same appendix tables in the October 1989 *World Economic Outlook.*

* Excludes debt owed to the International Monetary Fund.

[†] The 1990 and 1991 numbers are Fund estimates and projections.

produce for a reasonable rate of return.[8] In some cases overvalued exchange rates hurt competitiveness or low commodity prices make products hardly worth selling.[9] Also, increasing protectionist pressures in the world's most promising markets are cause for considerable complaint.[10]

These external obstacles to the recovery of the region's economies are real and significant. But they can not be adequately addressed independently of the need for fundamental structural reform of local economies. This is true both because the dysfunction of local economies in coping with these difficulties is inextricably related to far-reaching flaws in their own course and makeup, and because, politically, it is difficult to imagine that foreign actors will be sufficiently forthcoming if regional nations do not make a strong effort on their own behalf.

There is room for differences in emphasis in accord with local conditions and values—and disagreement over timing and particular means. But, in general, the kind of structural reform that is necessary must begin with substantial lessening in the costs of government to reduce chronically exorbitant public deficits which give rise to non-productive borrowing. Sound and stable currencies and the elimination of voracious rates of inflation is another necessary objective that would be furthered by such reductions. Cuts of this nature are never easy, always controversial and sometimes positively dangerous. But, in view of past experience, they simply must be made and maintained. Emphasis should be placed on reduction of

---

[8]It should be noted, however, that Latin America continues to export a growing percentage of processed goods to the Trilateral countries (as compared to traditional raw material, food and fuel sales) in spite of the present crisis.

[9]Sugar and beef are the two agricultural commodities most affected by trade barriers in the industrialized countries, accounting for about half of all the export earnings estimated to have been lost by developing countries due to protectionism in agricultural trade. These losses are concentrated in Latin America, where sugar and beef producers are estimated to have lost over $8 billion in potential export revenues in 1983 (1980 dollars). In that same year total aid programs from all industrialized countries for all developing countries totalled $22.5 billion. World Bank, *World Development Report, 1985* (London: Oxford University Press, 1985), p. 41.

[10]The complaint is only partially justified. In fact, many Latin American countries have made substantial progress in penetrating the markets of the industrialized world—especially that of the United States. On the other hand, the developed nations are significantly protectionist in many areas of particular interest to Latin America, including textiles, steel, sugar and other agricultural products—and certain light manufactures. In addition, intensifying trade contention among the world economic powers now sometimes catches Latin America in the middle. For example, it is generally acknowledged that the "Super 301" provision of the U.S. Trade and Competitiveness Act of 1988 was aimed at Japan—but that Brazil (and India) were also targetted by its application in 1989 so this would not appear to be the case. Also, the very success of Latin American exporters often precipitates a counter-reaction pushed by local producers in the markets they are entering—as Costa Rican and Colombian flower growers, Brazilian shoemakers and Mexican and Chilean vegetable producers can attest.

unproductive facets of bureaucracy, on eliminating subsidies to marginal services and unnecessary consumption (not to mention political employment and outright corruption), and on augmentation of reasonable and legitimate sources of income—like strict enforcement of universal, equitable tax collection. Vehicles for truly productive investment and the provision of necessary social services should be streamlined and protected, as possible.

In a more general sense, and for reasons other than cost, necessary governmental processes should be "debureaucratized" and made more efficient. Government, at all levels, should restrain its tendency to try to regulate private activity down to the most miniscule details. And the state should divest itself of unnecessary and grossly inefficient branches of activity—through some appropriate degree of privatization, if possible, or liquidation, if necessary. Much greater reliance ought to be placed on secondary capital markets (i.e., stock exchanges) as determinants of value, as vehicles for attracting domestic savings and foreign capital, and as mechanisms to facilitate privatization and debt reduction.

The restoration of general business confidence is fundamental to increasing local savings (including retention of flight capital) and attracting foreign resources to provide necessary levels of new, productive investment. Easing restrictions on foreign investment, simplifying bureaucratic procedures and protecting patents and copyrights could also go a long way toward attracting necessary capital and technological inputs. Lowering trade barriers, where practical, would encourage improved competitiveness of local industry and reduce inflation (while improving the quality of life); and lowering of barriers is necessary to secure reciprocal access to foreign markets. The basic issue before local governments is how to escape present burdens and mobilize the capital, technology and organization necessary to find a competitive place for their economies in the world economic community. Toward this end, the necessary inputs must be attracted and matched to areas of economic activity where a natural competitive advantage is enjoyed. At the same time, the resultant production must be effectively marketed both at home and abroad.

Clearly, these structural adjustment measures on the part of the Latin American nations must receive adequate and simultaneous external support—so as to promptly convert them from net exporters to net importers of capital. Presumably this process would first involve multilateral and other governmental sources of funds. The Inter-American Development Bank, with its profound knowledge of regional problems, would be the most appropriate center of the effort. With multilateral and other governmental institutions acting as a catalyst, private sector funds from abroad and local savings (including the return of flight capital) would be required to complete the process. What is necessary to resolve the region's now pressing problems is that a serious effort to achieve structural reform at the local level be met by an equally serious initiative on the part of the global community.

C. Social

In this area the central question facing regional nations is whether they can get ahead of a rising tide of social issues that is increasingly pressing in upon them. There is little question that, after general improvement over the course of the post-war period, social conditions in Latin America have deteriorated alarmingly in the more recent past. This situation has, unfortunately, come about at a time of rising expectations and growing politicization—producing predictable frustrations that threaten the fabric of the new democracies struggling to survive throughout the region.

The nations of Latin America and the Caribbean have long been struggling to overcome the social and economic underdevelopment of varying, but generally substantial, portions of their populations. The degree of success was very uneven from country to country and at differing points in time.[11] And high rates of population growth, uneven income distribution and rapid urbanization often set the process back. Especially troublesome have been persistent pockets of generalized deprivation like the Brazilian Northeast and the Indian communities of the Andes—and the proliferation of urban slums around almost all major regional cities. By and large, however, the percentage of the region's citizens lacking adequate health care, nutrition, housing, education, and other basic social amenities was probably decreasing for most of the post-war period—even if their absolute numbers remained the same or actually increased.

Continued—or if possible, more rapid—improvement presumed growing economies and adequate levels of resources available to local governments for ongoing investment in social infrastructure. Since

---

[11]For the first half of this century, virtually the entire populations of Argentina and Uruguay enjoyed living standards not noticeably different than those of Europe—but both countries have fallen far behind Europe in the period since that time. In Brazil, a large, First World middle class emerged in the post-war decades, but lives side by side with an enormous and growing Third World population. And in Haiti, traditionally poor social conditions have evolved in the direction of the horrendous during the Duvalier years and their aftermath.

the early 1980s these prerequisites to social progress have been generally lacking throughout the region—with predictable consequences. Although the rate of population increase has abated somewhat, the region's measurable social indicators have been falling for almost a decade now.[12] The region's "social deficit" in terms of caloric and protein intake, housing, health and education, transport and general social and physical infrastructure has clearly reached record levels. One additional result of these circumstances has been an explosion of both unorganized and organized criminal activities—particularly in certain major urban centers of the region.

No one can predict the specific political consequences of this situation, especially if it is allowed to continue indefinitely. Certainly, they would vary from country to country. But, in general, conditions of this nature certainly bode ill for the stability of local societies and the survival of their frequently fragile democratic institutions. In addition, they pressure local governments to take confrontational stands toward the international community and are capable of producing the kind of convulsions which, in the past, have often led to the involvement of foreign powers. When combined with the violence and general hopelessness these circumstances are prone to engender, they clearly portend intensification of the export of regional problems—in the form of illegal immigration, and, in some cases, organized criminal activity. For all these reasons, in addition to purely humanitarian concerns, the Trilateral nations should be acutely concerned with the deteriorating social conditions of the region.

D. Security

The fundamental security question facing the nations of Latin America and the Caribbean is whether they have the capacity—singly, or in concert, and possibly in cooperation with extra-regional actors—to forge an effective approach to present and future threats to the safety of their citizens and the stability of their institutions. A careful and substantial distinction must be kept in mind here between military security questions and matters which are essentially police matters. Many of the nations of the region currently face no appreciable security threat and/or have the ability

---

[12]Between 1981 and 1988, for example, educational spending by the central governments as a percentage of GDP appears to have decreased in almost every Latin American country for which data are available. Inter-American Development Bank, *Economic and Social Progress in Latin America, 1989 Report* (Washington, D.C.: IDB, 1989), pp. 60–61.

to cope with their problems on an individual basis.[13] But for others this is clearly not the case.

There is presently little in the way of a generally accepted and practically effective mutual security system in the region with respect to either military or law enforcement matters. Locally representative groupings and institutions like the Group of Eight, the Central American Presidents and the OAS tend to axiomatically recoil from unilateral U.S. involvement in such questions. On the other hand, countries that find themselves with problems which neither they nor their neighbors can handle in some cases want and expect decisive assistance, which, for the time being, only the United States seems able to provide.

At base, the civilian political and intellectual class of the region has great difficulty in coming to effective grips with practical security problems. Their historical experience and the nationalism of their peoples strongly incline them to oppose "interventionism" of any kind. At the same time, rigid segregation of the civilian and military spheres inside their societies tends to deprive local elites of much experience with, or even interest in, practical security questions. In fact, it is interesting to note that there exists practically no discernible school of *realpolitik* thought among the civilians of the region. The place for prudent use of security instruments in an overall policy aimed at safeguarding national interests and ensuring personal safety is often underestimated. And the level of knowledge and inclination to deal with such matters has historically been low.

The dichotomous notion that civilians deal with negotiations toward peaceful solutions based on laudable principles, while security questions are for the military or *in extremis* the United States to handle, is a dangerous one—particularly for the democracies of the region. In the first place, merely a propensity to negotiate, unsupported by at least the possibility of applied power, is generally ineffective in dealing with violent and intractable elements which are the essence of most criminal or politico-military threats to civilized democratic societies. And if negotiations fail, direction of more forceful means (or direction of the country for their application) should not necessarily fall into exclusively military hands as a result. Similarly, as a general rule, the United States should not be dragged into helping individual

---

[13]Nor (except for a couple of isolated cases) do Latin American military budgets, which were always modest and have been steadily falling in recent years, impose much of a burden on local finances. As a percentage of GDP, military spending is less now in Latin America than in any other area of the world. *The Military Balance, 1989–90* (London: The International Institute for Strategic Studies, 1989), p. 211.

countries against the wishes of other regional democracies. Such efforts have often proven to be difficult to sustain in the court of U.S. public opinion and complicate Washington's overall relationship with the Hemisphere—while at the same time distracting U.S. policymakers from the more general issues facing the region.

This discussion of regional attitudes toward security questions is not an abstract one. The region does face serious problems in this regard that can not be simply wished away. Indeed, a new constellation of security issues seems to be emerging that will be at least as troubling as those of the past. One eternal problem is the question of the continued presence of non-democratic regimes in the region. Haiti has yet to embark upon an irreversible transition to pluralistic democracy and may well experience serious trouble in so doing. Although signs are now hopeful in Central America, the nascent democracies of the Isthmus still face serious problems. And, of course, there is the seemingly intractable case of Fidel Castro, which is of particular concern because of Cuba's tendency to support armed subversion of neighboring governments. Finally, we can not yet rule out the possibility that some presently existing democracies will fall to dictatorship or anarchy in coming years.

Anti-democratic insurgencies will continue to provide the region with its most immediately pressing security issues. This has particularly been true when local governments were squared off against a communist-backed insurgency as has been the case in El Salvador. But even when international political motivations are less clear, as in Colombia—or practically non-existent, as in Peru—the potential for local carnage and escalation of external involvement is high. This is particularly true when radical insurgencies become involved with the emergent drug mafias in an effort to overthrow democratic government. In fact, it is this kind of warfare—as well as direct struggles against the *narco-traficantes* and their corrupting power—which will probably provide the greatest challenge to regional security in the 1990s.

Fortunately, there is little prospect for purely national conflict in the region for the foreseeable future. Likewise, conflict with extra-regional states remains a remote hypothesis, with the only real controversy of this nature (between Argentina and Britain over the Malvinas/Falklands) now apparently well on the road to accommodation. Likewise, local arms control problems do not appear to be a pressing issue, except in Central America, in view of radically reduced regional patterns of military spending. The nuclear programs of Brazil and Argentina that raise potential proliferation questions have also not been heard from recently—also probably for financial reasons. Still, the Trilateral countries should exercise caution and restraint in the transfer of sensitive technologies, and avoid arrangements which would facilitate local exports of weaponry to questionable destinations. In addition they should unanimously urge regional countries to subscribe to the Nuclear Non-Proliferation Treaty and complementary local arrangements, such as the Tlatelolco Treaty.

E. Foreign Policy

The basic foreign policy challenge facing the countries of the region is whether, individually and collectively, they can now articulate and successfully implement positive international strategies aimed at realizing concrete domestic objectives and forging appropriate roles for themselves in the wider international community of the 1990s. The historical record here is mixed.

Throughout most of the 19th Century, Latin American countries struggled among themselves in a number of contentious sub-regional systems—and attempted to draw economic benefit from, while fending off periodic intervention of, the major powers of the North Atlantic world. The end of that century and the beginning of this one witnessed the emergence of U.S. dominance in the Hemisphere and the forging of the Inter-American system that was its institutional expression. There were, of course, exceptions to this general trend. Residual aspirations toward Latin solidarity were evident from time to time; and the foreign policies of Mexico and Argentina stressed resistance, and occasionally opposition, to Washington's emerging role in the Hemisphere. In addition, Britain had partial success in retaining—and totalitarian Germany and Italy in forging, for a time—a certain presence in the region. But by the end of the Second World War the dominant position of the United States was substantially unchallenged and secure. The comportment of the nations of the region in the final stages of that conflict and in the early Cold War years largely conformed with this new reality.

Since the late 1950s, and especially since the 1970s, however, Latin America and the Caribbean have been coming out from under the shadow of the United States. This trend has taken various forms—including the transformation of Cuba and Sandinista-ruled Nicaragua into open antagonists of the United States in the context of the Cold War. In addition, the states of the region have become more assertive and less tractable to U.S. preferences locally. Since the 1970s, Washington has been unable to line up OAS majorities in support of its regional policies, and ad hoc fora excluding the United States—like SELA, the Group of Eight, and the Central American Presidents —represent efforts by local states to take responsibility for regional events into their own hands. Finally, on the wider international stage, regional actors have become more visible both individually and collectively—and other world commercial powers have inserted themselves more forcefully into the economic affairs of the Hemisphere, providing a certain counterweight to the position of the United States.

Nevertheless, the approaches of regional foreign policies to wider international affairs seem to have stagnated. This is both a cause and a symptom of the systemic crisis that has gripped the region over the past decade. Because of its great potential and strategic importance, Latin America had always had a surfeit of sometimes overbearing suitors. Thus, foreign policy focused on protecting the region from outside interference and bolstering the autonomy of local decision-making processes. These traditional efforts, though understandable and laudable, are seemingly exhausted—in large part by their own success.

Now Latin America's principal problem may be too little, rather than too much, international involvement in the region's affairs. The area's problems and attractive opportunities elsewhere in a very competitive global environment are causing many important foreign actors to lose interest—and this at a time when the nations of Latin America desperately need to insert themselves into the fast-flowing mainstream of international political and economic events. The present challenge appears to be that of building foreign policy agendas which attract and hold the constructive attention of the global community—particularly the developed nations and their private sectors.

This implies seeking out and building upon opportunities that are both attractive to important foreign actors and beneficial to local interests. It means, for example, demonstrating to Japanese investors that there exist opportunities in the region that are superior to those in East Asia. It means selling competitive products at competitive prices to Europeans who could get these goods elsewhere. And it means showing the United States that cooperative initiatives with regional nations will heighten American competitiveness (and, in other dimensions, protect Washington's security interests). Efforts to move regional integration beyond the symbolic level, in order to concretely strengthen the capacities of local actors, would be another imperative in this regard.

Agendas would thus shift from defensive abstractions to the positive and concrete. What do the U.S.-Canadian trade agreement and plans to create a single market in the European Community by the end of 1992 imply for Latin America? Where are the best opportunities for Latin American products and how are they best placed in the targeted markets? What needs to be done to defend Latin American democracies and how can Latin America obtain whatever external support is necessary to achieve this end? Would greater integration among the countries of the Southern Cone or the old Central American Common Market strengthen their respective national economies? And, if so, how do we achieve such integration? What needs to be done on the principal environmental questions? What can nations outside the region contribute in this regard? What has to be done to attract foreign investment and channel it into appropriate sectors of local economies? These are the kinds of practical questions that frame the issues for Latin American foreign policies in the 1990s.

V. Toward the Future: Recommendations for the Trilateral Countries

In order to forge a policy appropriate to the challenge that we now confront in Latin America and the Caribbean, the Trilateral countries must first come to accord the region the high priority which any rational calculation of our interests now requires. If this, indeed, is our conclusion, we should move promptly to define and implement a coordinated and effective blend of political, economic, social, security and diplomatic initiatives toward the region. This effort should be area-wide in scope and embrace all issues which significantly affect the interests of local societies and our own. Such a policy should be a positive and integrating one which emphasizes identifying and acting upon objectives which the industrial democracies stand for, and toward which the peoples of the region universally aspire. These goals should be sufficiently high to be inspiring, but sufficiently practical to be attainable. And the approach should be innovative and realistic—aimed toward achievement of concrete, mutually beneficial results in the near and medium-term future. Such an initiative will require close consultation with regional governments on a regular basis.

The achievement and preservation of stable, functional democracy throughout the region is the basic political goal shared by the Trilateral countries and the peoples of Latin America and the Caribbean. And unquestionable, effective support for democracy must comprise the cornerstone of any positive and successful policy toward the region. The promotion and sustenance of regional democracy can not be undertaken principally from abroad—but must count basically on the efforts of local societies and leaders. Still, there are certain measures that the industrialized democracies can take to encourage and support regional efforts.

First and foremost, there is the question of attitude and posture. The foreign policies of the Trilateral countries should demonstrate genuine interest in, and accord a reasonably high priority to, Latin American and Caribbean affairs. In word and in deed, we should provide frequent recognition of, and support for, local efforts to establish, perfect and sustain the practice of democratic government.

In more practical terms, we need to give expression to our preference for democracy with as many tangible benefits as possible for its practitioners. From a foreign policy standpoint, this means more frequent consultation with Latin America's democratic leaders on matters of mutual and general interest and the progressive integration of their governments into the network of constant contact already linking the industrialized democracies.

The industrial democracies should ensure that all their dealings reflect this decided preference for the regional democracies— particularly their aid, trade and overseas investment promotion policies. Specific attention should be devoted to providing and encouraging assistance that substantially contributes to the building of modern democratic institutions. This means emphasis on exchange programs that expose local leaders to ideas and practices that make democracies work more effectively and encourage regional cooperation. (The European experience with economic and political integration could provide substantial experience in this regard.) In this context, enhancing contacts and programs involving Trilateral and regional parliaments, judicial officials, scientists and technicians, businessmen, journalists, and military officers would be most useful. Beyond the sphere of government per se, linkages between political parties and relevant press, educational and research institutions can make an important contribution to both integrating Latin American democracies with those of the industrial nations and transferring the attitudes and skills required to perfect and sustain regional democracy.

The difficult and controversial questions arise, however, when individual local governments fall out of compliance with generally accepted democratic norms (especially if they show no signs of returning to such practices), engage in gross violations of human rights, and/or endeavor to export undemocratic systems of government through violent means. A limited number of cases of this nature are, and will probably remain, serious problem areas for Latin America and can not simply be ignored.

There is no easy answer here. Condemnation, ostracism, aid and trade sanctions, interruption of normal diplomatic relations, or stronger measures, even when sincerely aimed at promoting or defending democracy, are not to be embarked upon lightly. Ideally, the industrialized democracies, in close consultation, should strongly support the joint initiatives of the regional democracies in treating these difficult problems.

It is undoubtedly in the economic area where the most hard and potentially profitable work lies before us—not only to surmount the real and pressing dangers that are all too apparent, but also to realize bright opportunities that may presently seem more obscure. The new regional democracies need to function economically on behalf of their societies or they will fail. If these economies perform productively, however, the result would be of great benefit to the economic interests and political objectives of the industrialized democracies.

We must realistically appreciate the fact that the keys to resolution of the region's problems do not rest in any foreign hands. Old-fashioned statist economic policies, excessive economic nationalism, bloated and inefficient bureaucracies, imprudent borrowing, wasteful spending and outright corruption did much to land the nations of the region in the circumstances in which they now find themselves. No extraneous influence or effort to help can be successful if local governments are not willing to undertake the often difficult task of substantial economic reform. And many sympathetic observers would note with sadness that, as a region, Latin America seems to be lagging behind even the communist states in recognizing past mistakes and taking energetic, effective remedial action. There are, however, more and more exceptions to this pattern. Nations such as Bolivia, Chile and Mexico deserve special commendation for the courses of structural reform they are now pursuing.

It will, however, require more than the prospect of commendation from the Trilateral countries to help the nations of the region to reform and energize their lagging economies. Some of the necessary effort must come in the form of jawboning regional governments and societies on behalf of liberalization measures that the whole world knows hold the key to economic progress. Local pride and interests must be given due consideration. But, as in the case of democracy, talking up the virtue and necessity of economic reform and fostering exchanges of ideas and people to promote the process can help. This is a task which should not fall exclusively to the governments of the Trilateral countries; the resources, knowledge and enlightened self-interest of our respective business communities and other private institutions should also be enlisted in the effort.

More concretely, the Trilateral countries should pursue economic policies that are more cognizant of the opportunities which the region offers for mutually beneficial interaction and more helpful to prospects for the region's prompt economic recovery and future advance. It is important, however, to be clear, honest and realistic with our Latin American and Caribbean friends. As the economies of the Trilateral countries are of a basically liberal stripe, it is not our governments which will allocate resources of the kind and quantity that the nations of the region require. Only the private sector disposes of the capital, technology and expertise that are truly necessary. And, in practice, the business community will only commit these resources to those countries which have created the conditions where they can be productively and profitably employed.

But governmental policies can help to catalyze and supplement this natural attraction between resources and opportunities. The governments of the Trilateral countries should take proper cognizance of the substantial opportunities in the Latin American arena—and that recognition should be reflected in policies toward debt, trade, investment, the environment, and foreign assistance.

What is needed on the debt question is a series of simultaneous reciprocal actions from debtors and creditors alike. The regional countries must undertake real and effective structural reform. And their creditors have to respond with tangible measures that have the effect of alleviating the burden of debt service and facilitating re-ignition of the local economies. Because the circumstances of the debtor nations vary greatly and because no reciprocal action can be expected, or would help, until a clear commitment to reform is in evidence, this process can only occur on a case-by-case basis. But, once reform is in train, it is important that creditors respond in an effective and coordinated manner. Since the Trilateral countries are virtually synonymous with the creditors, our cooperation is crucial in this regard.

Debt-equity swaps are in some cases very helpful vehicles for debt reduction, since they are voluntary, facilitate privatization, and have the effect of keeping capital in debtor nations and strengthening local capital markets. (Remedying the historical weakness of local capital markets—including stock exchanges—and spreading capital ownership through innovative measures like Employee Stock Ownership Plans are two real benefits that could come out of the present crisis.) But, in view of the huge volume of the debt and the deteriorated state of many of the indebted assets and the political sensibilities of some countries, these swaps are not a universal panacea.

Broader, more comprehensive arrangements must be made. The accord with Mexico reached last year—and related agreements now being reached with Venezuela and Costa Rica—point in the right general direction. This approach, however, must be perfected, expanded and extended to other deserving countries as quickly as practicable. Mexico, obviously, has made a serious effort toward reform. And, in response, foreign private creditors were given the choice of (1) making new monies available equivalent to 25 percent of outstanding credits, (2) exchanging Mexican debt for new bonds with a reduced interest rate (fixed at 6.25%) but with the same nominal value, or (3) exchanging Mexican debt paper for new bonds with a reduced nominal value (65% of the old debt) but at commercial interest rates.

This arrangement may not have provided all the relief that Mexico wanted, or may in the future need. And perhaps the hand of the U.S. government was too heavy on the private bankers—which may discourage some of them from playing the role in the region that will be required in coming decades. It could also be argued that some debt-holding governments and multilateral lending institutions did not shoulder the responsibility or take the hit that they should have together with the private banks. But clearly something along these lines was required for Mexico and will be required for other regional nations if they are to revive their economies in the near-term future. The details of the deals can be amended and perfected on a case-by-case basis as we proceed down this road. Indeed, the Costa Rican and Venezuelan arrangements differ significantly from the Mexican accord and from one another.

In this regard, a new look, on the part of the Trilateral countries, at our banking laws and regulations and at relations with the multilateral lending institutions might help ensure more enthusiastic and general participation in this necessary, but sometimes painful, process. We should, after all, endeavor to assure that the burdens which are incurred are borne in an equitable fashion. The United States might learn from the European laws which, generally, allow for private banks to amortize loan losses over longer periods of time. And the Japanese might consider American practice which permits banks to build up large reserves against troubled loans. In addition, all the industrialized democracies might consider larger and more prompt contributions to multilateral lending institutions, if these institutions prove capable of making greater efforts with truly deserving debtors who are the object of intense treatment by the governments and private banks of the Trilateral countries. New and innovative possibilities should also be considered and examined. The

European Investment Bank might, for example, consider becoming a significant shareholder in the Inter-American Development Bank.

While Mexico is a good example of the general direction of future efforts, it is not a particularly representative case. The strength of its reform effort, its weight with the banks and its economic and strategic importance to the United States earmarked it above all others for prompt and effective treatment. Thus we may see great difficulty in moving beyond Mexico and a few other special cases.

This is where cooperation on the debt question among the industrialized countries becomes particularly important. And, frankly, greater leadership is now needed on this pressing matter from the governments of the Trilateral countries—most particularly that of the United States. Specifically, we should make necessary changes in our domestic regulations to facilitate debt relief, combine our efforts, and move quickly to accelerate treatment of deserving debtors with measures that provide clear and tangible benefits. Such an initiative would significantly advance the recovery of nations already making necessary efforts and offer important encouragement to nations like Argentina which are struggling toward real reform measures (and like Brazil, where an ambitious effort has recently been initiated). Prompt action now would also have the advantage of incurring any burdens in a sequential fashion—so that future candidates can be processed as they show results from reform efforts.

Trilateral trade policies toward the region may have even more long-term importance than the debt question—if we can ever get over this latter hurdle. Basically, both the near-term recovery of the local economies and their future place in the wider international economic community depend upon the industrial democracies further opening their markets to the region to the greatest possible extent.

The nations of Latin America, of course, have to do their part through structural reform, progressive liquidation of their own not inconsiderable protectionist barriers, and avoidance of other grossly unfair trade practices. As a general rule, they could also do a much better job in taking advantage of opportunities that already exist and more effectively promoting their trade around the globe. But as the generally prosperous pillars of the international economy, the Trilateral countries should take the lead and set the best possible example.

Despite much ongoing regional complaint, the United States has done a reasonably good job in this regard, particularly given the protectionist pressures generated by the very large trade deficits it has experienced in recent years. The protectionist threat has been largely kept at bay and, in fact, considerable tariff cuts have been negotiated with a substantial number of regional nations. In addition, innovative initiatives like the Caribbean Basis Initiative and the *maquiladora* program have broken new ground in exploiting mutual interests, providing greater trading opportunities for regional nations while enhancing the competitiveness of U.S. industries. The framework agreement through which the United States and Mexico are reciprocally reducing trade barriers is also a positive development—that is now giving rise to discussion of a more comprehensive free trade area concept between the two nations. The relative openness of the U.S. market in large measure explains how Latin America and the Caribbean have managed to survive the travails of the past decade. Still, there is more that the United States should be able to do in this regard, including prompt passage of improved CBI legislation and concerted attention to difficult cases of residual protectionism—especially to egregious cases doing great harm to the region, such as sugar and textiles. A reduction in the extent of borrowing of world savings by the U.S. government to finance its budget deficits would allow these savings to flow more easily to developing countries in Latin America and elsewhere, and also tend to reduce the U.S. current account deficit and the protectionist pressures associated with it.[1]

Europe and Japan have a mixed record in the trade area. If they wish to be of greater assistance to the recovery of the economies of Latin America and the Caribbean, they should take a hard look at how to improve market access for Latin American products, particularly in the critical agriculture area. In addition, they might consider initiatives based on the basic principle that economic activity in the region can be increased while their own competitiveness is enhanced through essentially subcontracting manufacturing and assembly activities that no longer make sense in their own high-wage economies. Also, to the extent that Japan and certain European nations can reduce their own trade surpluses with the United States, they will facilitate a

---

[1]"Japan and parts of Europe have large surplus savings. The natural destination of these savings is those countries that are poised for development, but lack adequate capital. The debt crisis of the 1980s has inhibited the flow of private financial resources from Europe and Japan to most of those developing countries. Instead, these savings have flowed in large amounts to the United States. There is nothing intrinsically wrong with that, if it contributes to U.S. growth. But attractive U.S. yields are due in considerable measure to a large budget deficit, rather than to exceptional opportunities for real investment. So there is good reason for believing that the debt crisis and large U.S. government borrowing combined are disturbing the natural and desirable flow of capital in the world." Shijuro Ogata, Richard N. Cooper, and Horst Schulmann, *International Financial Integration: The Policy Challenges* (New York: Trilateral Commission, 1989), pp. 5–6.

continuation and expansion of Washington's liberalizing initiatives toward the remainder of the Western Hemisphere.

In fact, given emerging international opportunities to devote enhanced attention to the constructive task of strengthening the economic ties among the democratic community of nations, the GATT negotiations or exploration of a new general trade initiative ought to be vigorously pushed forward by the Trilateral countries. In any such effort to liberalize and expand commerce on a global basis, the nations of Latin America and the Caribbean should be among our foremost considerations. Their interests would be best served by efforts to reduce First World protectionism in areas like textiles, steel and, of course, agriculture. Serious thought should also be given to triangular trade opportunities among Latin American nations, Trilateral states and third countries in Eastern Europe and the Pacific Rim.

In addition to debt and trade, the international investment policies of the Trilateral countries are also a significant factor for the nations of the region. Of course, it is only the private sectors of the industrial democracies that possess the capital, technology and managerial resources necessary to make a significant impact on the economic future of the region. And to attract these resources, local governments will, in the final analysis, simply have to create the kind of business conditions that are necessary to interest them. But all governments also conduct programs aimed at promoting and facilitating investment overseas. Mindful of both long-term business opportunities and more general foreign policy considerations, our governments should not neglect Latin America and the Caribbean with respect to commercial staffing of our respective embassies, trade missions, insurance facilities and the like.

Finally, on the aid front, the industrialized democracies should do what we can to defend and advance general foreign assistance levels and channel as high a percentage as possible in the direction of the region. Care must, of course, be taken that programs are effectively administered and intelligently applied. In this regard, it is important to recall Latin America's problem with overblown, self-serving bureaucracies. To the extent possible, aid funds should be targeted toward potentially productive projects and the service of genuinely humanitarian needs—rather than paying the debts of hopelessly inefficient local institutions. It should be kept strongly in mind that poorly targeted and wasteful programs are not only ineffective, but also provide an invitation to cuts in foreign aid by resentful legislatures. Also, as a matter of principle, the allocation of aid among local countries ought to show a decided preference for those which practice democracy and are engaged in economic liberalization.

Trilateral countries should seek niches in areas that match Latin America's most real and pressing needs. Europeans—Spain, in particular—might wish to concentrate on the reform of local legal and judicial systems that is so necessary for greater social equity and economic progress. The Japanese obviously have special expertise in technological training and are increasingly interested in environmental questions. Canada seems to have a special proclivity for providing social assistance. And the United States has obvious abilities in the agricultural area, while its extensive private sector presence might be better mobilized to provide better training in modern business practices.

Local bureaucracies are not the only ones about which donors should be wary. Better results for the money can often be achieved by channeling funds through Private Voluntary Organizations (PVOs). In general, private organizations ought to be encouraged by the Trilateral governments to supplement official foreign assistance for humanitarian, educational, training and professional exchange purposes. Here again, in addition to purely humanitarian programs, private attention should be focused on efforts which contribute to the building of effective democracy, economic reform and fostering understanding between local societies and the Trilateral world.

What can be accomplished in the social area depends basically on what local governments do with the resources that they command, including the foreign assistance from Trilateral countries discussed in previous paragraphs. As mentioned, the increasingly critical nature of the situation in the region requires that the levels of this assistance be maintained as high as practicable. And the alleviation of social distress should figure among the top priorities of both local governments and foreign donors. Special attention should be given to pressing problems of food, health, social infrastructure and education—especially in those countries where the governments clearly do not possess the resources to undertake the necessary effort. Rethinking and streamlining aid efforts to ensure that the greatest real impact is achieved from available resources is also a very important matter.

The Trilateral countries, especially the United States, will undoubtedly be involved in difficult regional security issues. Where possible, all the industrialized democracies should support the initiatives of regional states to find the often elusive keys to peace and stability. But such efforts must begin from a willingness on the part of the Trilateral countries, in consonance with their own values and capabilities, to sustain local democracies against violent and intractable elements whose objectives run contrary to liberal and civilized government.

These principles must apply, at the present moment, most particularly to the ongoing Central American crisis and to the dangerous situations that are now emerging in Colombia and Peru. In general, Latin America and the Caribbean need to form a new and more effective regional security system, bolstered, as necessary, by a common effort on the part of the industrialized democracies. Such a system must offer real and practical prospects of general support for members of the local democratic community menaced by contemporary threats of terrorism, organized crime and subversion. And the Trilateral countries should be willing to back any such effort, to the extent that a consensus of regional actors thinks necessary. Serious thought about new institutional mechanisms to update or replace OAS-Rio Treaty arrangements is clearly in order—including consideration of some form of multinational police force.

Simultaneously, the members of the North Atlantic Alliance should be thinking about a new global role for this Alliance under changing international circumstances. This might logically entail greater involvement in the defense of democracy and the promotion of stability in the Third World. Also new institutional arrangements on the drug issue—linking the European Community, other Trilateral countries and the wider world—ought now to be seriously considered. Latin America would be a prime candidate for closer cooperation in these regards, both because of the difficulties which regional states have had in confronting potentially destabilizing trends and because, frankly, a good deal of this violence is still fueled by forces with which many local actors—especially the smaller ones—can not hope to cope effectively by themselves.

In foreign policy terms the nations of the region need to forge effective strategies that produce concrete benefits to local societies by bringing them into full participation in the world's democratic community. That community, in turn, should now be sensitive to the opportunity to significantly broaden its scope—and to the dangers to its interests if conditions in the region are allowed to deteriorate further. The Trilateral countries need to educate the Latin Americans on how our policymaking mechanisms really work—and the regional actors must become more effective in lobbying the industrialized governments with respect to their interests and concerns.

At present, the relationship between the region and the industrialized democracies tends to be defined by the problems that afflict it. All there seems to be are disputes and disagreements, especially with respect to debt, drugs, trade and the pace of local reform efforts. In the case of the United States, this is often aggravated by divergences over political and security questions. The result is that Latin America has lost considerable interest from, and influence with, the Trilateral countries in recent years.

By and large, Latin American foreign policies tend toward abstract idealism rather than effective promotion of practical initiatives. Meanwhile, policymakers in the Trilateral countries are discouraged by local prospects and increasingly distracted by more positive developments elsewhere. As a result, we lack a practical, positive and mutually agreeable agenda for the future of the relationship.

Partial exceptions to this discouraging pattern exist. And they should be studied to determine what is required more generally. Mexico and Chile, countries with very different recent experiences, provide the best examples in this regard. Both of these nations have come to the conclusion that practical initiatives based upon comparative advantage and prospects for mutual benefit are the most reliable way to gradually, but surely, advance national interests. As a result their foreign policies seek to identify and pursue concrete, practical objectives in which foreigners share an interest. This process progressively engages rather than repels policymakers and businessmen of other nations—enlisting their ideas and concrete contributions for new common ventures.

In light of ongoing events like the U.S.-Canada Free Trade Agreement and European Community plans for 1992, we should be discussing with Latin American nations their place in a dynamic new international economic order. Politically, Latin America's trend toward democracy must be sustained and we should be working with regional leaders to show the successes of socio-economic reform under free political institutions to the remainder of the Third World. We should now be building on the hopeful peace prospects in Central America by turning our attention to the economic recovery of the area. And a host of challenges in such diverse areas as debt, trade, competitiveness, resource availability and the environment beckon the policymakers of the Trilateral countries and the region to productive dialogue.

Latin America is still an area of great promise—if the policies of its governments are pragmatic and if foreign nations demonstrate the interest that the current constellation of dangers and opportunities so fully warrants. What is required from the foreign policies of both parties is realism, respect, reciprocity—and detailed attention to finding the concrete trade-offs that solve existing problems and uncover bases for expanded, mutually beneficial cooperation in the future.

ENTERPRISE FOR THE AMERICAS INITIATIVE
June 27, 1990

The preceding report has highlighted the imperative for significant efforts by Trilateral governments and private sectors on behalf of the economic recovery of Latin America. As the authors were finishing their final editing, the President of the United States, on June 27, 1990, announced his plan for the region—the Enterprise for the Americas Initiative.

Although many of the details of this initiative are lacking at the time of this writing, it is comprised of three basic parts. The *trade* component posits a comprehensive Free Trade Agreement between the United States and all of Latin America as a long-term goal. But, realistically, it appreciates that the process can only occur gradually—as the nations of the region think themselves prepared for an arrangement of this nature and as the United States, itself, is able to accommodate such a large and varied array of new partners. The accord with Canada took several years to reach, and comprehensive negotiations with Mexico are only now really beginning. But the United States has now served notice that it is ready to begin additional talks with any interested regional nation (or group of nations which has associated for purposes of trade liberalization) toward bilateral framework agreements as interim steps toward the comprehensive, long-term objective of free trade throughout the Western Hemisphere. In the shorter term, the trade component of President Bush's initiative places strong emphasis on hemispheric cooperation toward successful completion of the Uruguay Round of GATT negotiations—in which the concerns of the Latin American countries should be given special consideration.

Secondly, the Enterprise for the Americas Initiative focuses on *investment*—and the urgent need to mobilize both foreign and local capital for the purpose of reigniting regional economies. The key is to encourage the countries of Latin America and the Caribbean to pursue policies that will attract and facilitate the necessary new capital flows. Toward that end, the Initiative proposes a lending program at the Inter-American Development Bank to provide both technical advice and financial support for privatization and liberalization of investment regimes—possibly in conjunction with the World Bank. Additionally, in a parallel effort, a new five-year multilateral investment fund would provide up to $300 million annually in grants to support specific, market-oriented investment policy initiatives and reforms aimed at attracting foreign investment; would be administered by the Inter-American Development Bank; and would complement existing lending programs at the IDB and World Bank. The United States would contribute $100 million yearly, and would look to the E.C. countries and Japan to provide like amounts.

Finally, the Initiative would provide additional support for *debt and debt-service reduction*. Specifically, it proposes that the IDB become an additional source of enhancements under the present debt strategy. These enhancements would be used to back specific transactions negotiated by Latin American and Caribbean countries with their commercial banks. And, as in the case of the IMF and World Bank, the availability of these resources would be tied to economic reform efforts. In addition, to address the problem of official debt, legislation will be proposed to permit a substantial reduction and restructuring of existing U.S. concessional loans to Latin American and Caribbean countries with serious debt-servicing problems. In this area, specific provisions will be made to allow payments on restructured debt to be made in local currency to be placed in trusts to support bona fide and significant projects aimed at preserving the regional environment. Authority will also be sought to allow the sale of a portion of outstanding bilateral commercial credits under the U.S. Export-Import Bank and Commodity Credit Corporation programs. It is expected that these measures would produce a substantial reduction of concessional U.S. Agency for International Development and PL-480 claims, particularly for the smaller countries of the region. Finally, the Initiative pledges to seek maintenance of new foreign assistance flows to the region at least at current levels.

Obviously, many of the details of this Enterprise for the Americas Initiative remain to be filled in. Problems may emerge with the U.S. Congress—especially over the enhanced support for the IDB, the forgiveness of official debt, and the trade negotiations that are envisaged. The European countries and Japan have yet to speak on their possible contributions to the new multilateral investment fund or their willingness to engage in parallel efforts to reduce official debt. And, of course, many other good ideas for additional action may be suggested both within and beyond this Initiative.

But it does seem to the authors that President Bush's new initiative speaks very much to the general thrust of analysis and recommendations contained in our report. We, therefore, urge its energetic and comprehensive implementation by the United States government—and its concrete support by the E.C. nations and Japan. All in all, it seems to be a substantial and serious stride toward the goal of a healthy and vibrant Latin America restored to effective partnership with a free and prosperous global community of nations.